Divine Legacy

God's Riches for the Servant Heart

Blessings!
Betty Jane Begley

Divine Legacy

God's Riches for the Servant Heart

Betty Jane Negley

Treasure House

An Imprint of
Destiny Image® **Publishers, Inc.**
P.O. Box 310
Shippensburg, PA 17257-0310

"For where your treasure is
there will your heart be also." Matthew 6:21

ISBN 1-56043-273-X

For Worldwide Distribution
Printed in the U.S.A.

Treasure House books are available through these fine distributors outside the United States:

Christian Growth, Inc.
Jalan Kilang-Timor, Singapore 0315

Successful Christian Living
Capetown, Rep. of South Africa

Omega Distributors
Ponsonby, Auckland, New Zealand

Vine Christian Centre
Mid Glamorgan, Wales, United Kingdom

Rhema Ministries Trading
Randburg, Rep. of South Africa

WA Buchanan Company
Geebung, Queensland, Australia

Salvation Book Centre
Petaling, Jaya, Malaysia

Word Alive
Niverville, Manitoba, Canada

This book and all other Destiny Image and Treasure House books
are available at Christian bookstores everywhere.

Call for a bookstore nearest you.
1-800-722-6774
Or reach us on the Internet: **http://www.reapernet.com**

Betty Jane Negley
6373 Lincoln Way West
St. Thomas, PA. 17252
717-369-4400

I echo the words of Psalm 26:7:
"That I may publish with the voice of thanksgiving,
and tell of all Thy wondrous works."

It is my desire that the contents of this book will inspire others to find the joy and fulfillment of the Second Blessing experience with its accompanying power and anointing to touch the lives of many.

I dedicate this book with love
to my beloved husband Paul
and our children.

Acknowledgment and Gratitude go to:
my brother
Professor O. Richard Forsythe—Editor
and to my daughter
Katrina Negley—Artist.

Endorsements

The Lord's call and guidance in our lives are unique to each one and yet there are clear patterns which repeat over and over. Paul and Betty Negley had no idea that God would one day lead them to foreign lands nor that they would experience intense physical suffering along with misunderstanding and occasional rejection among their colleagues of the Kingdom. They did not anticipate extended separation from their children and grandchildren. Nor did they expect to be involved in minstries of healing or deliverance. Yet all these things have been the lot of these two modern Anabaptist servants. Their quiet confidence and humility commend them to all who meet them. It is a confidence founded on God's faithfulness, the authenticity of the Scriptures, and the abiding presence of the Holy Spirit. It is a humility born out of continued reinforcement in their experience that "without Him we can do nothing," that He is Lord, and that we are privileged servants and members of His family.

This book provides a glimpse into the faith journey of one family, not unlike many others, and yet uniquely and distinctly different. There is material here to inspire the seasoned veteran and encourage the novice. It is a story worth reading and sharing with friends. This account of God's ways in the lives of two twentieth century pioneers should find its way into many Christian homes and church libraries.

Daniel Yutzy

When Jesus walked this earth, he chose some ordinary men to teach and disciple in the things of God. They ate with Him, traveled with Him, slept with Him, and learned how to live the way of God's Kingdom.

Following His death and resurrection, Jesus sent the Holy Spirit on the Day of Pentecost to empower the disciples, men and women who had gathered in the upper room, to be witnesses of the power and the glory of God and to do ministry of reconciliation in the name of Jesus!

Since His departure to Heaven, He has transferred to His disciples and all who would believe the gift of the Holy Spirit to do His work as stated in Luke:

The Spirit of the Lord is upon Me, because He hath anointed Me to preach the gospel to the poor; He hath sent Me to heal the brokenhearted, to preach deliverance to the captives, and recovering of sight to the blind, to set at liberty them that are bruised (Luke 4:18).

Betty Jane Negley has beautifully explained how God called her and her husband, Paul, from ordinary Anabaptist beginnings to do extraordinary things with their talents and spiritual gifts to the praise and glory of the Lord! Not only have they been used to touch lives in the United States, but their ministry has extended beyond these borders, personally and through the lives of their children.

I have watched the Negleys in ministry for more than 20 years. I admire their humble, simple faith and their quiet spirit that teaches, ministers, and leads by example. The Lord is still looking for willing persons to do His work. Anabaptists and others will be challenged by reading this story. I recommend this book for your Christian growth.

R. Eugene Miller, Pastor
Longmeadow Church of the Brethren
Hagerstown, Maryland

Contents

Introduction

The fresh crisp breezes of the new day greeted me as I stepped onto the porch and scanned the skies. The rising sun was pushing back the darkness. As this new day dawned, I felt intensely God's love for me and my family.

The September air was filled with that special aroma of freshly fallen leaves, still damp from the early morning dews. My husband Paul had already left for work. Our daughter Rosanna, a registered nurse, was on her way to the hospital. Our youngest child, Katrina, had just been sent off to school with a quick blessing. As I watched the school bus pull away, my heart seemed especially full of joy.

Perhaps the joy came from my anticipation of the Prayer and Praise Bible Study Group that would be meeting that morning. I was still musing over this as I turned to my prayer reminder board near the kitchen sink. One by one I lifted up those special needs of the persons God had laid upon my heart: the missionaries, several orphans, various ministries, and those who were sick and suffering and looking to me for intercession. Somehow I still could not fathom the unusual joy and excitement that permeated my spirit that morning.

By ten o'clock two ministers' wives and I arrived at the little Nazarene church in Shippensburg, Pennsylvania. Our special speaker that day was a petite lady from near Camp Hill, a professional musician and singer. I had heard her teach from the Bible previously, and I knew she was a real saint of God. The meeting opened with a time of praise and worship as the musician's fingers moved deftly across her autoharp. Her soft angelic voice began to worshipfully sing from the nineteenth chapter of the Book of Revelation. The Holy Spirit provided the music for the words.

It was absolutely astounding! Just as the Holy Spirit spoke to John with revelation many centuries ago, now I was about to receive knowledge. As she sang the word *write*, I felt as if a shaft of great power came from above and pierced my heart. Just as John knew he was commissioned to write that last great book of the Bible, I also knew God was placing a call on my life to write of the Glory of His Kingdom, to reveal and make known to the sons of men His mighty acts and the glorious majesty of His Kingdom.

As the Spirit of God swept over me, I wept in His Mighty Presence. I will never forget those awesome moments and my commission to write. As I realized what a tremendous and impossible task was being placed before me, I also remembered that with Christ nothing is impossible.

For nearly four years, many had encouraged me to write of the marvelous things Paul and I were experiencing in our walk in the Spirit. Since I had no formal education in writing, I had told the Lord that if He were instructing me through these requests, He Himself would need to show me personally in some definite way. That day in September I experienced His profound direction, and I will never doubt its authenticity.

Because of my great love for my precious Lord Jesus and my gratitude for all that He has blessed me and my family with, I now move out in obedience to His divine will through His command: "Write."

Chapter 1

The Canopy of Christ

In the state of Maryland, just across the Mason-Dixon line, my parents, Albert and Alma Forsythe, struggled to make a life for themselves on a huge farm. Interestingly, the farm was built on this line: the house sitting on Maryland soil, while the barn extended several feet into Pennsylvania. This was the line of freedom in the days of the Underground Railroad, the days when escaped slaves fled for their freedom to Mt. Parnell, a mountain peak of the Tuscarora mountains in Pennsylvania.

My parents experienced long hours of toil on the farm and spent numerous freezing winters in the drafty stone farmhouse. Its many rooms were impossible to heat in those days before the luxuries of furnaces and indoor bathrooms became part of our lives. At that time, a tenant farmer received half of the farm's crops for his wages. This meant a lot of long, hard days of work and a dependency upon God for favorable weather so that they could raise enough to feed the family and possibly lay a little money aside for that proverbial rainy day.

My brother Kenneth was born in 1925, and I was born on March 31, 1927. Our family remained on this farm several years until my father had an opportunity to move to the community of Lemasters, Pennsylvania.

My earliest memories come from those days after we moved to this area. These include those years during the worst time of the

Great Depression. Soon after our arrival, a bad drought brought great hardship to our family and all farmers.

Because lime was used in farming to improve crops and increase their yield, my father built a lime kiln and burned lime for himself and the neighbors to supplement our income. I remember one morning when he hitched up the horses to deliver lime, Kenneth and I wanted to ride along on his delivery. It was a blustery winter day; and when we arrived at the home, we children were quite cold. The lady of the house took us in and had us warm our hands and feet at the front of her big, black cookstove. Little did I know I would someday marry her youngest son and that this woman would become one of the most cherished persons in my life.

Four more children were added to our family during the five years we lived in Lemasters, close to the Tuscarora mountains. Each child was received as a blessing from the Lord. I remember one day Daddy remarking to Mamma that some man at church had noted our nice family and commented on a certain Scripture, "Happy is the man that hath his quiver full of them." In later years I discovered this quote was from Psalm 127:3-5a:

> *Lo, children are an heritage of the Lord: and the fruit of the womb is His reward. As arrows are in the hand of a mighty man; so are children of the youth. Happy is the man that hath his quiver full of them.*

In the fall of 1933, Galen Albert was born. He was a beautiful baby with soft brown curls, the first of my brothers and sisters that I was big enough to rock and to help with.

In preparation for that winter, we buried the cabbages, turnips, and apples in a pit in the garden, which was formed somewhat like a cistern. The hole was lined with straw to prevent freezing. Whenever we needed any of these things throughout the winter, we would carefully lay aside the boards and layers of straw and make our selection for the meal. In those days mother dried corn, peas, and beans and canned other things to last us through the winter months while Daddy spent long days sawing and splitting fire-wood in the woods. The corn, although mostly "nubbins," was gar-nered in carefully, for every grain was precious. Our half of the meager harvest was stored in the crib next to the barn. Although our lot was difficult, we were grateful, for we had land on which we could grow food. During these days of the Great Depression, many who were not farmers had to stand in long lines to receive food to keep their families from starvation. Through these early experiences, we were taught to receive everything with thanksgiv-ing; and I cannot remember any complaints of dissatisfaction from my family about our lot in life.

About the middle of November, my mother came down with a sickness that required hospitalization. Galen was only six weeks old. *How could we ever get along without Mother, and where would we get money to pay the hospital bill? We children could carry the wood, bring in the water, feed the chickens, and gather the eggs; but how could we tend the fires and dry the baby?* My young mind was flooded by thoughts of the impossible. However, Daddy arranged for his youngest sister, Aunt Suie, to come and stay with us. What a busy household for an eighteen year old to take charge of!

She did a fantastic job, and how we loved having her with us! It was certainly a good thing Grandmother had taught her how to cook, for we always seemed ready to eat up all the corn cakes and pudding or whatever she prepared and set on the table for us. Yet there was something she could not supply: a mother's warm em-brace. Each day that need became more magnified until we all felt the same way. As the days dragged on, we grew quieter and even our appetites lagged as our homesickness intensified.

Eventually, Thanksgiving Day arrived, but our hearts were no longer longing for the turkey gobbler. Instead, we were filled with a new kind of yearning, for that was the day Mother was to come home. Near noon, a strange looking vehicle pulled up to the gate of our white picket fence. I don't think anything in the world could have kept us back as we rushed out the front walk and stood gazing upon our mother's face as the ambulance attendants carried her into the house. Mother was still very weak and sick, and we tiptoed around the house for fear she would have to leave us again. It was like heaven just to have her in the house where we could touch her once more. Those kisses from her were so wonderful that we slipped to her bedside as often as we possibly could. As the weeks passed she grew stronger, finally Aunt Suie returned to her home and her own heavy chores, which included the care of her invalid and blind sister Ruby. Aunt Ruby experienced a spinal injury from a fall as a small girl, which eventually caused her paralysis and blindness.

The winter was cold with lots of snow. Each day Daddy prepared our sleigh to haul two 10-gallon cans of milk to the creamery several miles away. We took turns accompanying him, and he would tuck the black bearskin lap robe around us. How we loved the crunching of that fresh crisp snow as the sleigh's runners cut new tracks through the deep drifts! It seemed that our horse Prince felt the excitement of it all, too, for he always took off at a trot, nearly upsetting us as we rounded the big curve near the creamery at Williamson. Our fingers and toes tingled, and our cheeks stung from the wintry winds, but the ride was exhilarating!

Near the end of January that year, we began to take our turns with bad colds. Because antibiotics were not available in those days, Mother treated us with common home remedies. She greased our chests with melted lard and a bit of kerosene; or if the cough seemed extra bad, she would add tar to lard and apply it to our chests. Mustard poultices were used for severe colds. When anyone was sick, a couch was moved near the round-bellied living room stove and he was told to stay there to keep warm. So many prayers and so much tender care were part of our treatment that we nearly enjoyed being sick. However, when the baby became sick and his tiny body grew hot with a high fever, we sensed this was no ordinary cold. The doctor was called, and we learned he had pneumonia. The following day, six-month-old Galen lost his battle for life.

I keenly remember this first encounter with death. As I pushed a chair beside the diminutive satin-lined casket and climbed up to see our baby's sweet little face, I thought surely this must be just some kind of sleep; he looked so peaceful. Silence pervaded the house, broken only by occasional somber voices. Galen's body was prepared at home for burial, as was the custom in those days. Many neighbors and relatives came to offer their sympathy and extend a helping hand, for Mother was still quite weak. A neighbor, Mrs. Reeder, made him a tiny satin dress with embroidered pink roses on the front. Accentuating his soft brown curls, the dress etches a bittersweet memory into my mind, one of despair, courage, stoic acceptance of God's plan in our lives, and the incredible love which existed among neighbors when adversity struck.

The day of the funeral service arrived, and we all followed close behind the white casket as it was carried into the brick church on the hill. The minister said something to assuage our grief, and we sang "Safe in the Arms of Jesus, safe on His Gentle Breast." With this, my heart knew a new comfort; for if this is where our little baby had gone, he surely would be all right there with Jesus.

Springtime came. Warm weather arrived, and spring showers carved rivulets in the earth that had been parched by the previous summer. With renewed hope and faith, my parents began another year. Fields were plowed and corn was planted again.

We children contented ourselves with the usual activities that go with the pre-school years. One afternoon, wanting something different to do, Kenneth and I decided to play "house" in the turkey gobbler's coup attached to the end of the barn. We found a cardboard box to serve as our table. Using old canning lids for dishes, we decided to cook dinner. Of course, we also needed small sticks and a match to make our cooking fire. Just as the fire was started, Daddy happened on the scene. This was undoubtedly the hand of God, even though it certainly put an end to our fun.

The horror on Daddy's face and the understanding that we had nearly burned down the landlord's barn were a deep lesson in obedience for our memory catalog.

That fall I accompanied Kenneth to Lemasters' two-room school. Like most children, I remember more about our lunchtime games and the box of dinner Mother packed for us than the reading, writing, and arithmetic lessons.

Every Sunday we traveled the three miles to the long, brick church on the hill. Erected in 1870, it consisted of one large room. At either end of the room were elevated seats, which were usually used only by the Sunday school classes or for seating the larger crowds that came on special occasions like Love Feast or revival services. Kenneth would lead me to our Sunday school class, wiggle up onto the bench, then pull me up beside him. The teacher had a long pointing stick that she used as she explained the biblical heroes on a flip-tablet of pictures. She showed us Moses in his ark in the bulrushes, Daniel in the lion's den, angels coming down the heavenly ladder in Jacob's dream, and many other biblical pictures. These held a deep fascination for me as I received my earliest Christian training.

In those days we visited only relatives, close friends, and neighbors. And how we looked forward to those trips to Grandpa and Grandma's house! Grandpa Forsythe lived in Maryland. In our 1924 model Chevrolet, those 20 miles seemed a real trip. Because cars at that time were not equipped with heaters, four would sit in the narrow back seat with the black bearskin lap robe tucked snugly around us.

After one such visit, we were on our way home at night, coming down a steep hill near Cearfoss, Maryland. At the bottom of the hill was a humpback stone bridge. At the beginning of our descent, Daddy discovered he had no brakes. *How would we ever make the curve to cross the creek bridge?* This is my first recollection of prayer; I knew as well as all of our family that only Jesus could keep us from going into the water. Not a word was said, but we were all praying and holding our breath. Daddy somehow managed to clear the curve, and we were across the creek! I remember my parents giving thanks to God for many years for His protection on Creek Hill that night.

Chapter 2

Moving Day

My dad was determined to improve the family's circumstances and kept his eyes open for a more productive farm. He had heard of one near the village of Shady Grove. After looking it over, he decided this was our next home.

Moving day arrived on March 31, 1934, my seventh birthday. A new home, what an exciting birthday present! With the exception of the beds, bedding, the heavy cookstove, a table, and sufficient food for our morning meal, all our household possessions were loaded onto two farm wagons the day before the move.

In the morning all our neighbors arrived bright and early to help us. Some of the men drove the cattle along the 20 miles of back roads leading to our new home. Others drove the teams of horses that pulled the wagons of furniture. Still other relatives and friends drove cars to carry the women and children. The farm machinery had already been moved earlier that week.

As we arrived at our destination, we were filled with great excitement. We ran from room to room, exploring our new house and trying to decide which room would be assigned to us.

During this time, the adult members of the "flittin' party," as it was called then, were busily engaged in unloading the heavy iron stove from the wagon. The cookstove weighed about 600 pounds, thus requiring every man's help. It was past noon, and everyone was showing signs of hunger. However, the linoleum needed to be rolled out on the floor before the stove could be placed. After that came the hasty erection of the black stovepipe and a quick trip to the woodpile. The fire was soon blazing, and the chicken noodle soup that had been prepared earlier for just this occasion was heated. The long table and the chairs were placed in the kitchen, and soon the men entered, bringing the tall, brown cupboard. Women were unpacking dishes and setting places at the table. This made the house already seem like home as smells of chicken and homemade noodle soup filled the air.

Soon the table was surrounded with hungry men and boys. Grace was said for the meal consisting of soup, potato salad, baked beans, ham, pickled eggs, dried corn, fruit, and many kinds of cake and pie. The women and children ate last, freeing the men to do the heavy lifting and many tasks yet to be accomplished. In the afternoon, carpets were placed, beds erected, and feather mattresses and linens were brought out of boxes until all was readied for a good night's rest. By evening it really was our home *and* my very own birthday present!

Our seven years at this farm yielded many memories for me. Soon after we arrived, the man who owned this farm died. We had a good working arrangement with his widow and their son, Adam, who lived beside us in their own house.

It was here that Kenneth, Vernon, and I learned to milk cows. Our responsibilities included pumping water for the cows and horses from the cistern. Around and around went the handle. Each of us counted 100 turns before we exchanged places to catch our breath and rest. I remember watching the bulging sides of the cows and wondering where they could be putting all that water. We were always responsible to keep the wood box filled and help keep the garden free of weeds in the summer months. In the summer when the pasture was short, we were expected to "watch the cows," when they were let out of the barnyard to graze by the side of the road.

We had fun times, too, as blackberries and red raspberries were often growing along the fencerows at this season of the year. They were a delicious treat on a hot summer day and broke the monotony of our chore.

As my brothers grew older, they were able to drive the horses and help harvest the alfalfa and clover crops. Each year at the close of summer harvest, our parents planned a special evening of homemade ice cream and invited those who had helped with the work to come enjoy it. A party with ice cream was a real treat! In the fall, the whole family husked corn from the shocks and gathered it into the barn. We often made games out of our work, like seeing who could husk the most corn. And when Daddy could afford it, we were each paid a nickel a shock. A shock of corn consisted of several armfuls of corn cut while still green and stood up together to dry. A nickel a shock was a big incentive to encourage us to learn how to earn and save our money.

One year when my parents seemed to be doing better financially, each of my brothers was given a pig to raise, while Annabelle and I each received 20 chicks. We were responsible for caring for our projects. I am not so sure it was a good bargain for my parents; they had to pay for the feed. Then when the hogs and chickens were big enough for killing, we sold them to our parents and helped to eat them! That's what you call a good deal for the kids! We all enjoyed our projects until the day our pets had to be slaughtered. Sometimes we needed to balance our thoughts against our appetites as we looked at the fried ham and the roast chicken on the middle of the table.

However, the money in our hands from selling the hogs and hens was a really wonderful experience. Although our parents taught us to save the largest amount of it, we were allowed to spend a portion on a toy, an act that required much thought and decision. My choice was a Shirley Temple doll. We long remembered that day in the toy shop and the joy our parents shared in being able to give us such valuable lessons that money could never purchase.

Each winter, snow covered the ground nearly all the time. Often the roads were completely impassable. There were times when we could only determine where the roads were by the fences.

Sometimes we even drove our horses over top of the fences where the drifts were high. We shared a lot of fun while sledding on our three sleds. When there was an extra good frozen crust on the snow, we would also use an old piece of tin roofing. With the one end bent upward, it provided room for three or four of us to ride down steep hills with tremendous speed. I am sure the canopy of God's protecting hand was over us many times, for this was really very dangerous. We often darted beneath the barbwire fences at the bottom of the hill.

Summer activities included hours of fun for Annabelle and me as we played with two new families of kittens that arrived every spring. They slept for hours in the baby carriage and allowed us to push them through the yard in the hot sun. It is amazing how well they put up with all of our antics of motherhood.

We loved to slide down the big straw stack, especially just after the black, steam-powered threshing rig pulled away from our farm. We often played games in the barn, and we loved to jump down from the big logs in the barn into the fresh, sweet-smelling hay. This created a near disaster one afternoon when we slid down into a hole between the great jags of loose hay. Because each child followed closely behind the other, each of us slid down, down into our little prison. We were all trapped. Realizing our hopeless condition and knowing we dare not try to get out for fear of pulling the loose hay down upon us and smothering, we started a screaming medley.

It seemed like an eternity until we heard a voice. Mr. Byers, our landlord, occasionally checked the premises to see if all was being accomplished as he desired. Praise the Lord...he had chosen that day and time to look around. His long, red beard had never seemed so beautiful to me as when he stooped to the edge of the hole and pulled each of us to safety.

It was at Clay Hill that I learned to love school. I finished first grade the year we came to this area. The two-room brick building accommodated eight grades, four in each room. Miss Edith was our teacher, a strict disciplinarian, yet she demonstrated much love and kindness to all who would follow her instructions. When someone defied her regulations, their penalty was a swat across the knuckles with a heavy ruler. When this was not sufficient, Miss Edith gingerly escorted the little rebel to the porch where Mr. Davidson, who taught in the other room, was called to deal out further punishment with a strong paddle.

Multiplication tables were drilled into us until we felt as if we would say them in our sleep. Then there were all the hours of effort given to the "push and pulls" and the "ovals" of the Peterson writing method, which was used in penmanship classes. Each of us was required to produce copies of meticulous perfection.

With four grades in one room, it was easy to listen in on the other classes. When my work was finished, I would become bored, and I found myself listening to the next grades' lessons and following along with their work. At the end of the year, my teacher talked to the county superintendent, who gave me permission to skip the sixth grade. The following year I found myself absorbing the studies of the eighth grade students. I was able to keep up with their assignments; but at the end of the year, I experienced one of the hardest blows of my life. The superintendent had begun to frown on this type of promotion, and he would not consent for me to be in high school at so early an age.

I was not only heartbroken; I became very bitter toward this man. My teacher understood my feelings and tried to compensate by allowing me to help him with extra activities and securing advanced library books for me to use. It took many years of Christian maturing to learn how to relinquish this bitterness.

Chapter 3

Jesus—My Lily of the Valley

When we moved to Shady Grove, we attended a church two miles from our home. Built by our Christian forerunners, circa 1855, Hades Church was a long, gray, limestone structure, a typical Brethren-designed church with upper and lower levels.

For several years my father was the custodian of this church. I loved to go with him early in the morning to kindle the fires in the two round stoves that sat at each end of the long room. I helped to sweep the bare wooden floors and dust the seats while the fires slowly warmed the sanctuary in preparation for the service. Even though the huge room was empty and cold on these winter mornings, I sensed there was some sacredness about the place.

Daddy was given a love offering of $20 a year for his janitorial services. Through this I learned that Daddy was rewarded in some way that was better than the receiving of money. Now, many years later, I still respect janitors of churches, and I believe their call to serve God is one of the most underappreciated tasks that are done in the Lord's work.

The basement of the church was used for meals, which were served as part of the observance of Love Feast. The Love Feast and communion service were carried out as identically as possible to the meal Jesus ate with His disciples in the upper room just before going to the Garden of Gethsemane. Love Feast was conducted semi-annually. During the horse and carriage days, members from long distances would stay overnight in the attic of the church, which was partitioned to accommodate both men and women.

The church's bench-like pews were designed so that the back of every third one could be flipped to create a table between every two seats. These tables were used only during the Love Feast observance. Saturday and Sunday meals were served in the basement to all who attended. The preparation for this sacred event began early Saturday morning. A wood fire was built in the old-time furnace, which had space for two large black iron kettles. The first was used to keep a supply of hot water for cooking and for the washing of feet. The second was used to boil one or two lambs, depending on the number of members in the congregation. Only members were permitted to participate in this holy communion and Lord's supper commemoration.

The meal consisted of plates of the cold sliced lamb and vegetable-sized bowls of hot broth with rice, accompanied by bread and butter. Four persons dipped soup from the same dish at the meal, symbolic of the significance of common sharing.

Preaching began early Saturday morning and lasted throughout the day. The holiest part of the day was the Saturday evening memorial of Christ's death. Tables were readied for the meal and remained covered with cloths until the ordinance of foot washing was observed. For this ordinance, men sat on one side of the room and women on the other. Each person girded himself with a long towel-like apron and washed and dried the feet of the person to his right. After this a basin was passed for washing hands.

When this part of the service was finished, the meal was eaten quietly and reverently. Next the scriptural admonition to greet one another with a holy kiss was observed (see 1 Cor. 16:20). Some of the younger children would get the giggles as the noise of kissing lips resounded throughout the sanctuary. Even the smallest of sounds seemed intensified in the reverential stillness.

Next came the partaking of the bread and cup. Long narrow strips of home-baked unleavened bread were passed to each person, who, in turn, broke a one-inch portion for the person sitting next to him. This was eaten in silence, as each deeply meditated on how Christ's sufferings and anguish had brought us great blessings. Just as the bread was prayed over by the officiating minister before being distributed among the members, so also was the cup of grape juice with the entreaty that God might bless it from a common use to a holy purpose. The common cup was then passed to all the communicants for each to take a sip.

We were dismissed by a prayer of benediction and the singing of a hymn that corresponded with the disciples' experience.

The communion service was a sacred time for recalling what Christ had done for us through giving His life on Calvary so that we could be released from our sinful nature. Underneath the people's serious countenance glowed a joy. I wanted to know more about that something that radiated happiness. How did one find that something?

In December 1935, the congregation scheduled a two-week revival, and we were asked to keep the visiting evangelist at our home. Like many other Brethren men in the ministry, Albert Nisewander never accepted the title of *Reverend*, considering it to be too holy a designation. Brother Nisewander, as he preferred to be addressed, was a man nearing 60, with a long, fluffy, gray beard hanging over his upper chest. He loved children, which he demonstrated through the special attention he gave us. Toward the late afternoon and early evening, we tiptoed around the house so that he could pray and seek God for a message for the evening service.

One night as the invitation to accept Christ was given, the congregation was singing the old hymn "The Lily of the Valley." As I listened, something began to happen deep within my heart and spirit.

The Lily of The Valley

I have a friend in Jesus, he's everything to me,
He's the fairest in ten thousand to my soul;

The lily of the valley, in Him alone I see,
All I need to cleanse and make me fully whole.
In sorrow he's my comfort, in trouble he's my stay,
He tells me every care on him to roll.

Yes, He all my griefs has taken, and all my sorrows borne;
In temptation he's my strong and mighty tow'r;
I have all for him forsaken, and all my idols torn
From my heart, and now he keeps me by his pow'r.
Tho' all the world forsake me, and Satan tempt me sore,
Thro' Jesus I shall safely reach the goal.

He will never, never leave me, nor yet forsake me here,
While I live by faith and do his blessed will;
A wall of fire about me, I've nothing now to fear,
With his manna He my hungry soul will fill.
Then sweeping up to glory, to see his blessed face,
Where rivers of delight shall ever roll.

Chorus
He's the Lily of the Valley, the bright and morning Star,
He's the fairest of ten thousand to my soul.

C.W. Fry and Jas. R. Murray

I felt an urgent pounding in my chest. The Holy Spirit was convicting me. Surely Jesus was the one I wanted to follow and have for my best friend. Jesus would never leave or forsake me, and someday I would see His blessed face. In accordance to the custom of the church, I rose to my feet to signify my decision to accept Christ as my Savior and become a member of the church.

I was sitting with my mother, who began to cry. I looked at her and wondered what was wrong. *Had I done something she didn't like?* Through her tears she gave me a sweet smile and squeezed my hand, assuring me that everything was all right. After many years I, too, would grasp the inner joy that illuminates the spirit when a loved one is born into the family of God.

My heart was filled with new joy and peace, the like of which I had never known before. I felt a settled knowledge of being accepted by God. I was prepared to face the future, knowing any wrongdoing in my life was now forgiven.

Several evenings later my brother Kenneth also made a decision to follow the Lord. Brother Nisewander gave my brother and me each a New Testament and a satin Bible bookmark with a table grace printed on it. He admonished us to read from our New Testaments daily and to pray often to the Lord for our relationship with Him to grow.

On January 2, 1936, seven of us who had made application for church membership were taken to Falling Spring, just east of Chambersburg, to be baptized by triune immersion. There were snowflakes in the air. Mother had dressed us warmly and placed layers of flannel under our clothes to cover our backs and chests so the water would not reach our bodies so abruptly.

Even though I was very cold, I remember promising God that I would shun satan and all his pernicious ways and that I would endeavor to follow Jesus all the way. The minister prayed for the Holy Spirit to come into my life as he laid his hands on my head before leading me out of the water. I believe that I received the Holy Spirit *in part* at this time.

> *In whom ye also trusted, after that ye heard the word of truth, the gospel of your salvation: in whom also after that ye believed, ye were **sealed with that holy Spirit** of promise, which is the **earnest** of our inheritance **until the redemption of the purchased possession**, unto the praise of His glory* (Ephesians 1:13-14).

The Greek rendering for the word *earnest* is a pledge, or down payment, a part of the purchase given in advance as security for the rest.

Near the end of December we were invited to Grandma Forsythe's home for a Sunday dinner. We had fun shooting marbles on the dining room floor and visiting in Aunt Ruby's bedroom where we all sat around talking about the usual family concerns. Aunt Ruby busied herself crocheting many pretty things in spite of the fact that she was both blind and bedfast. Even though her fall on the cellar steps many years earlier had resulted in the paralysis of her legs, her hands were constantly doing something.

Aunt Ruby often asked those coming into her room to tell her the color of a yarn, whether it was the pink or the blue that she was using to make a baby sweater. Sometimes if I was alone with her in her room, she would read to me from those strange braille books with huge pages and tiny dots pressed in them. Once I asked her what it was like to be blind, and she tried to tell me how dark it is when there is no light. I felt so sorry for her, but she always seemed happy and told us how much God loved her, for each year God sent her a pair of wrens to build their nest and sing from the pear tree just outside her window.

There was another unusual person in Grandma's house: her sister, Aunt Georgie had come to live with them from Pittsburgh. Uncle Mart, Aunt Georgie's husband, had been a wealthy man who owned a cigar factory. However, when he died, she was left alone and childless. She was what we called a "society lady," for she had never had to work or handle her finances. Consequently, when she was left alone in the world, she was unable to manage, so she came to live with my grandparents. She brought many pieces of beautiful furniture with her, including a glass cupboard of lovely china dishes, her sterling silver, and a silver tea set on a tea cart that sat at the end of the dining room. Grandmother's parlor became Aunt Georgie's parlor with her furniture and grand piano along with a picture of her and Uncle Mart. The early days of their lives were lived in their mansion with maids to do all the household chores. I loved to go into her bedroom and sit beside her on the velvet-covered chair and watch her comb her lovely, soft yellow hair. Her mahogany poster bed with its heavy white woven bedspread spoke to me of storybook luxury. In the evening she always seemed to be in another world, for she would dress up for dinner in the most exquisite lace-trimmed dresses left from her former elegant lifestyle.

I thought Aunt Georgie must have been very rich from her appearance. However, I was later to learn she was only living with memories. They were all that were left of a huge inheritance her lawyer had swindled away from her before she was aware of her plight. Through all this she never became bitter, but remained a sweet and wonderful aunt whose memory I still cherish.

We spent Christmas Day that year in Maryland with our Grandma Forsythe. This was also the winter we had the largest snowfall ever recorded in Franklin County. As we left our Grandma's house, the sky was overcast as if a great blanket were about to descend on the earth, and there was that heavy dampness that forewarns of a storm's approach. Birds were flying about in great frantic circles as if they knew they must find food, for their meager winter supply was about to be cut off.

As we left for home, it began snowing and blowing. By the time we reached Pennsylvania, a genuine blizzard was in progress. Daddy worked hard to get us as near home as possible, but we finally became stuck in a snowdrift. We had to walk a distance before we reached home. It continued to snow, but the amount that fell was impossible to measure because the wind whipped the snow into great drifts. Daddy helped us to reach home then returned to the car with a horse to help pull it free from the snowbank. In the process, he became very wet, cold, and chilled.

A few days later Daddy came down with a severe cough and high fever. Mother's tender care and home remedies proved ineffective; we sent for the doctor. He returned every day for several weeks, despite being unable to reach the house without walking a great distance because of the drifted roads. We appreciated Dr. Buckingham's constant care, but as my father's condition turned into double pneumonia, all seemed hopeless. He lay in delirium for many days. Mother refused to leave his side and sat by the bed in a chair. She did not go to bed for two weeks. My heart nearly broke as I studied the worried lines of her face. And once again I realized the necessity for intense prayer for my father's survival.

We children helped all we could, considering our ages; but we were still too small to take responsibility for milking cows, feeding horses, splitting firewood, or doing all the work involved in farming. Fortunately, we had many kind neighbors who came to help us. Since the roads were impassable, they brought us supplies of food by horseback from the Shady Grove store.

Weeks went by and still we prayed and looked to God to spare our father. Little by little the fever began to drop, and Daddy began to recognize Mother and each of us. It was so good to see him sitting up in bed and eventually become strong enough to walk about and pass his approval on the work that had been carried out at the barn by our loving, helpful neighbors.

Six long weeks had passed, and the roads were still tight with drifts when we received word that a family up the way was sick and had no food or wood. Mother and Daddy filled a sack with potatoes, flour, corn meal, sugar, and apples. He saddled a horse and rode up the road with the supplies, so grateful to be well enough to give someone else a helping hand after so many had helped us.

Toward the end of February or the beginning of March, the state organized a crew of local men to shovel open the roads. The 15 to 20 men worked several days to remove the 12-foot drifts from a gully near our farm lane.

In addition to the snow and general winter problems, we experienced a continual outbreak of infectious diseases. We had measles, mumps, and the chicken pox in rapid succession, with one or two of us children sick at a time, until all five of us had a turn. The school notified the Public Health authorities, who were always a week late in putting up a quarantine notice on people's doors. This meant no one could go to any public place and thus bring risk to others by exposing them to the disease. The quarantine for measles or scarlet fever was 21 days. It was like being in prison all winter! How I detested seeing those signs tacked on our door! I felt as if I now understood how the lepers of the Bible days must have felt when they had to go about continually crying, "unclean."

Almost every family had a similar story, especially where there were big families. Those long hours were times for memorizing poetry and reading the books that the school library allowed us to have. But with the scarlet fever epidemic, they were afraid the books would also be a source for the transferal of germs. Consequently, no new materials were brought for our studies during that time.

We entertained ourselves as best we could. We played dominoes and checkers and shot marbles. We played a game called "cat's cradle," using a string that we passed from one hand to another. Our toys were mostly homemade, created from spools and whatever was available. Because Mother was artistic as well as creative, she had some neat ways to cut a whole string of dolls or other fancy designs from one large sheet of brown paper by a special method of folding.

The Saturday night bathing procedure was a never-to-be-forgotten experience in those days without heated houses or bathtubs. Five neat piles of clean clothes were arranged on the couch. The tub was placed behind the pot-bellied living room stove. The fire was made extra hot until the belly of the stove glowed red. One by one we took our baths. Hurriedly we stripped off the "long johns" and took a fast dip in the tub, all the while being very careful not to back against the stove as we grabbed for our fresh underwear.

This room is also where we dressed for bed. Our bare feet fairly flew up the steps and back the carpeted hall as we popped into our feather beds with one lunge. We usually pulled our covers up over our heads, leaving only a breathing space to allow the crisp cold air to get down to our noses.

Before jumping out of bed in the morning, we would study the artistry of Jack Frost on the frozen window panes. What beauty as dozens of tiny frosty designs transformed the frozen crystals into fancy castles and other fairy designs.

We bought our groceries from a truck that had been converted into a grocery store. We called it the "store on wheels." Mother would sell her basket of eggs to the grocer and use that money to buy groceries. We really looked forward to the truck coming each week. All five of us would mount the back steps into the narrow isle between the shelved sides. One particular section held our special attention, for it contained varieties of penny candy. Each of us was given two cents with which to make our selection. There were lollipops, sugar babies, bacon strips, licorice strings, peppermint sticks, and three kinds of lozenges: chocolate, peppermint, and tea-berry. There were also tootsie rolls, chocolate drops, and hard candies. Our parents taught us to be grateful for one piece of candy when two could not be afforded.

Those childhood years of playful activities and fond family memories passed swiftly in spite of many of the hardships of the depression. The greatest obstacle of my first year of high school was overcoming my bashfulness and becoming accepted in this larger group. Many of the students were town children, and I felt inferior, shy, and uncomfortable. I abhorred this feeling of inferiority and determined that I would do something about it. I decided to do all I could to be a friend to others. I was completely unaware that there were many who felt as I did and, like me, desired to be accepted by someone else.

My efforts paid off, and I soon found myself with several girls I especially enjoyed. One was Alice Brumbaugh, who wore her long brown hair the same as mine. Our long braids were entwined around our heads by our mothers each morning. I was surprised one day when Alice took me for a walk to show me where she lived, and I discovered that she lived in one of the biggest houses in town. It was a lovely white house, huge and impressively sitting among tall oaks and flowering forsythia and lilacs in an enormous lawn. Alice was a brilliant girl and loved her studies as much as I, and we were soon sharing girlhood dreams and ambitions.

By the following spring, Mr. Byers, our landlord, had an uncle who wanted to rent his farm; we were now in need of tearing up the roots that had become so deeply embedded in those seven years at the Byers homestead.

My best childhood memories come from the various experiences of this time of my life. Much of my character and the foundation for my future walk as a Christian was established during this time. I began to learn the importance of faith in God through prayer. The stabilizing security of a godly inheritance through the lives of my parents and grandparents was molding my life. It was also this environment that helped me to become a born-again child of God at the age of nine.

Even though my understanding of Jesus Christ was limited in these early years, it was sufficient to bring the blessings of peace in my heart and a longing to tell others how wonderful it is to have Jesus as your Savior.

Chapter 4

Divine Intervention

The steps of a good man are truly ordered by the Lord (see Ps. 37:23), for we were able to rent another nice place near Waynesboro, Pennsylvania. On this farm there was a lovely yellow house, and just below it flowed a quiet stream of water through a green meadow. It was a beautiful farm. The meadow ground was very rich; however, many of the acres were rocky and hilly.

My brothers enjoyed the stream; they built dams in the summer and set traps for muskrats in the winter. When the stream froze over, we would ice-skate on it. I also loved to spend a free afternoon or evening watching the flow of rippling water.

On Sunday evening, December 7, 1941, we were sitting in the living room enjoying some radio programs when we were shocked to hear the newscaster announce there had been an attack on Pearl Harbor. Our country attacked! our ships, our men! We were stunned, as were millions all over the country. Just how would this affect our lives? It would be years before anyone could determine the extent of tragedy and suffering that followed this eventful announcement and brought on America's involvement in World War II.

These are the years I would like to forget—as though they never existed in my life. However, every life cannot consist only of good, but must also contain sufferings, sorrows, and disappointments. Therefore, unpleasant though they were, even these years served God's purpose for my life.

All men under 40 were required to register for the draft, even those with large families. Daddy was in that group, and later Kenneth was required to register when he turned 18.

The older men were encouraged to go to factories as the younger ones went into the service. So Daddy took a job at Pangborn Corporation in Hagerstown, Maryland. This made for long, hard days with his farming operation; the dairy herd had to be milked before leaving for the factory. The field work was done in the evenings and on Saturdays.

Kenneth married and started to farm a small place, but he was drafted shortly after and sent to Fort Belvoir, Virginia. I remember the strange thoughts I had when I accompanied his wife Opal and their daughter Vonnie on visits to the barracks. The military air of order, which was felt everywhere, was appalling to me. I also pitied the young men and those families affected. One could see the loneliness, homesickness, and anxiety on every face. My heart ached for them.

I had dated my high school sweetheart for a year when he enlisted into the military just before graduation. At that time the government did all they could to encourage young men to enlist at the earliest possible age. He was assigned to California, which seemed like the other side of the world in those years when trains moved slowly and there were no jets. Like most girls in the same situation, I accompanied his family to the town bus station for our final farewells. Would I ever see him again and would he change as so many of the others I had heard about? In their loneliness, many of the men turned to drinking and were unfaithful to their wives and sweethearts.

Soon after getting out of high school, I took a job in the engineering department of a factory tracing blue prints. It was a tedious job, requiring much patience and a steady and skilled hand as I sat at that table for long hours at a time.

Like thousands of other girls, I wrote letters and dreamed of peace. Time and circumstances matured and changed many of us. I was among the many whose sweetheart found new interests to ward off the frustrations of being far from family and loved ones.

Our wedding arrangements were almost completed, and the long-awaited furlough was only a few weeks away when I received a telegram saying that he had received other orders and would not be coming home. It was a terrible shock; and even though the other reason was given, I sensed that he could not go through with the wedding.

It took several years before I came to understand that this disappointment could be endured. I learned that the Lord had spread His canopy of love over me and that this divine intervention had been fully in my favor. As I look back, I can see that this was one of the greatest blessings God has ever bestowed upon me. How wonderful that our loving heavenly Father can see the end of our lives from the beginning! This young man, although well respected, had not wholly committed himself to the Lord; and my God had other plans for my life. I can see the importance of praying for several years that God would protect me from marrying a man who was not a Christian in the fullest sense.

Kenneth was transferred to Texas after his basic training. There he was trained to build bridges ahead of the troops on their way to combat zones. Daily we prayed that God would intervene and keep him from going to the battlefront. One day he was called before his superior officer and presented a medical discharge. His papers contained no explanation of the medical problem, and to this day we do not know the reason for the discharge. He had fallen arches but at that time many who had flat feet were being sent overseas. Praise God for His mercy and answered prayers!

On the evening of September 2, 1945, we were invited to the home of our factory supervisor for a picnic. While we were eating on the lawn, fire sirens began blowing and church bells began ringing. We realized something unusual was taking place and by radio we heard that a cease fire had been announced! The war was over! What a public celebration we had as the townspeople made a bonfire in the center of town and danced and sang for hours. Unfortunately, the scars of war were never to be completely forgotten, for many men had given their lives for that glorious freedom and the ringing of those bells.

These years of uncertainty and distress created a desire for something different in my life, although I was not sure what it was. Was it that I was not satisfied with my work, or was it the desire to be loved and to love that was giving me this unsettled feeling? I had dated quite a few men; several of them were fine Christians who had proposed marriage to me. Somehow I just could not feel any one of them was God's choice for me. Perhaps I would never find a marriage partner; maybe God had something other than this in mind for me.

One day at work, the department head had one of his many temper tantrums and flew into a rage. He acted as if he owned and controlled each person under his supervision, and I had had enough. I told him I would be leaving. When he tried to tell me I was too valuable to the company and could not leave, I promptly told him it was too late for him to show me that now or give me flowery speeches.

I decided to use the money I had saved and enroll in the Waynesboro Business College. I enjoyed my studies and felt a peace about going to school. Once more I began to feel fulfilled and happy as if the Lord were leading me.

About this time I experienced a fervent desire to be doing something definite in church work. One night I visited a church in the neighborhood where a lady gave a message in chalk art. Her picture portrayed one of my favorite hymns, "Jesus, Saviour, Pilot Me." She was a talented artist, and I was deeply impressed with her presentation of the gospel message.

Because I had always enjoyed art, I talked to the lady after the services. She encouraged me to let the Lord guide me in the work. She advised me of the materials I would need and where to purchase them. Daddy constructed my first easel, and I experimented and studied the books on chalk artistry that I was able to secure from the local Christian bookstore.

Some months later I was asked to do my first public drawing for the Shining Light Youth Conference. At this time I had little confidence that I could produce anything worthwhile for an audience; but because of my desire to work for the Lord, I accepted the invitation.

I was hoping for a bright, sunny evening for my illustration since I had not been able to purchase an electric color wheel like Miss Meyers had used to focus on her completed drawing. This light was essential for a professional and dramatic effect.

The day for the conference arrived, and with it came all the heavy, dark rain clouds the sky seemed capable of containing. I was quite distressed to say the least! I was so nervous that I lost my dinner. By evening there was no hope for a weather change, and I lost my supper as well. My frustrations were more than I could control, and I cried out to the Lord, "If this picture amounts to anything, You alone will have to make it so, for I must have light and I have none."

The time came for my part of the program. I chose to illustrate the hymn "Let the Lower Lights Be Burning." The young man who was to accompany me as a soloist had almost completed the song; and while I was finishing the harbor scene and lighthouse and putting the moon and its reflections in the sky, a glorious light flooded my picture. It was as though my hand was moved by an unseen power. I could hear people in the audience whispering, "Where is that light coming from?" Praise God, He had parted the clouds in the western sky, allowing the beams of a low-hanging evening sun shine in exactly on one small area. Those glorious rays of light illuminated my drawing for a few moments and shone upon the soul of a handmaiden who had a deep desire to serve her Master and follow His footsteps. As I took my place in the pew, the clouds moved together again and the darkness grew as intense as before. To this day that experience gives me faith to believe God for great things.

This was the first of many opportunities to use chalk art as a tool in child evangelism and adult ministry. Even after 40 years, I still find it necessary to depend on Him for a fresh anointing and inspiration for each picture.

On another occasion I was asked to minister to a Junior Church assembly. I accepted the invitation reluctantly and almost canceled it, for it was out of state and I had been told I would possibly be speaking to 12 to 15 children. I felt guilty for reconsidering. I felt as if the Lord had told me that He had opened the door and that I was not to think of the sacrifice.

At the close of my presentation, I felt impressed to give an invitation for anyone who might want to accept Christ as their Savior. Out of the 30 children who had come to the service, seven of them made decisions to accept Christ.

I was glad that the pastor's wife had been sitting in the classroom and saw for herself that the Holy Spirit had called the children. She suggested I take them across the hall for a time of instruction. They entered ahead of me and were kneeling in a circle and holding hands when I entered. Each one began confessing what he was experiencing before I spoke a word. It was absolutely beautiful to see the Holy Spirit working so mightily in these precious young lives. One of the boys, who appeared to be about 12, told of how he had come into the church that morning feeling that something was wrong. But now, he stated that he understood that it was the Lord speaking to him. His little face shone with the joy and excitement of someone who has been truly born again.

All my opportunities to witness have not, however, ended with the same triumphant note of power. Unfortunately, I have often quenched the Holy Spirit and failed the Lord many times.

When I was 20 years old, I worked for a Jewish couple in a ladies' apparel shop. Mrs. Goldberg was a clever business woman. Underneath her ability for making money, there was also an unusual warmth that touched my heart as she seemed to be reaching out to me for some answers. Yet I never had the boldness to verbalize to her my Christian joy and love for Jesus.

Her husband nicknamed me Angel, and he teased me several times about unloosening my long brown hair, as it made me more like the name he gave me. I was embarrassed at his request, and I did not have the discernment of the Holy Spirit to understand that he too was reaching out, seeking to fill the longing in his soul that only Jesus can satisfy. Soon after this he died from a heart attack and never learned that any lovely thing he saw in me was there because of the Messiah, who he believed was still to come to the Jews. For many years his wife continued to send me Christmas gifts. When I finally found the courage to explain that Jesus was truly the Messiah, she was too old and deaf to hear or understand. My heart nearly breaks when I think of that lost opportunity. Over the years I often wondered where the apostle Paul's boldness to witness came from and just how he acquired the ability to stand before kings.

When I finished my business education, I accepted a job as a private secretary for two Christian businessmen who owned and operated an electrical store and contracting business. I was happy with this position and earned $20 a week. After six months, I received a raise of $1.50 a week.

That job afforded me many opportunities to witness. One Friday evening the men had gone out for their meal, and a drunken man staggered into the store. He began to tell me of his hopeless state and his need for help. Although some would believe this man was only making the usual drunken scene as a plea for sympathy, I have never been able to console myself that the Lord had been requiring more of me at that moment than I offered—that I could have done more to lead him to Christ.

Satan also seemed to be aware of my longing to serve the Lord. I think he laughs at our inabilities and failures in addition to putting road blocks in our path to render us ineffective.

During July and August of 1947, I felt tired and listless. I also experienced numbness in my arms. After much doctoring and dental x-rays, they discovered the remaining root of a tooth that had been extracted several years before. The root had abscessed, and the infection was draining into my system. After the removal of the old root, every day for two weeks the socket was packed with medication. It took months to recuperate from all the poison in my system.

One evening in my bedroom during this time of physical weakness, I felt a strange heaviness move over me and a smothering sensation. I was frightened and could not discern what was happening to me. Then a strange thing occurred as my spiritual eyes were opened: I saw many little demons dancing with glee in a circle around me. The elf-like creatures were gray with hideous, sneering faces, which seemed to be saying to me, "You are trapped and we have control over you." A heinous laughter erupted from each of them.

I ran downstairs to my mother, trembling and hysterical as I told her what I was experiencing. I knew that the adversary was seeking to destroy me completely—in body, soul and spirit. Ephesians 6:12 says, "For we wrestle not against flesh and blood, but against principalities, against powers, against the rulers of the darkness of this world, against spiritual wickedness in high places."

Mother prayed with me as she held me close, and those demons were forced to move beyond my visibility. I know they are real, for I saw them with my own eyes. I praise God for a Christian mother who knew the One who can put satan's demons to flight.

I am grateful for God's mercy and revelation as He has given me understanding of the spiritual reality in satan's kingdom and of the potential the saints have to be victorious in battle.

Chapter 5

The Lord's Choice

October 19, 1947, was a gorgeous fall day. The air was filled with fluttering leaves in all shades of yellow from the maple in front of the white brick house in Shady Grove, which had been our home for three years. Shady Grove was a quiet village, consisting of about 70 houses, a post office, store, a church, and a doctor's office.

Daddy and Mother already left for church on that particular Sunday evening, and I was waiting for my date. My heart was racing with excitement and anticipation, for I had dreamed of this date for several months. I was dressed in my newest rust-colored wool creation I had finished the day before. As I waited, I snipped the last yellow rose of the summer and pinned it to my shoulder.

Promptly at seven o'clock, I answered the knock at our door and invited Paul Negley into my home and heart. Paul was a handsome 20-year-old man, with black wavy hair, brown eyes, and a crease in his chin. His face was etched with godly character and kindness. He possessed a gentleness that made him a true gentleman. He lived at Lemasters. He was the son of a prominent farmer and a member of the Upton Church of the Brethren. This was the same church I had attended as a child. We had both attended Lemasters school. However, neither of us remembered each other, for I had moved away at the end of my first year. Paul and I had become acquainted at a youth conference in 1946.

We had an enjoyable evening together, and I was impressed with his thoughtfulness and courtesy. Before leaving, he asked me if I would like to go with him to the Welsh Run Revival services the following Sunday night. Needless to say, I was pleased to accept this second date.

This congregation had a member who had been ill for some time. He was a farmer who had a lot of corn still in his field waiting to be husked. The youth group decided to have a corn husking party at his place to help get the corn into the crib before the winter cold arrived. That Thursday night I went with Paul to the husking party. It was a crisp and windy moonlit night. Mr. Etter's son drove us on a farm wagon to a field near the creek where rows of corn stood in shocks waiting to be husked. Each couple was to husk out the corn on their shock and put it on a neat pile. It was a custom that if there were any ears of red corn available, one was secretly placed beforehand in each shock of corn. When the ear was discovered, the boy was allowed to kiss his girl. Our shock did not contain a red ear; therefore, this intimacy was not to be an embarrassment in this stage of our new relationship. Being a farmer, Paul was very adept in pulling down the husks and removing the ears swiftly. He easily made up for my inability and speed, since it had been years since I had any practice at husking.

We finished our shock ahead of some of the others and stood talking behind some corn fodder for protection from the wind. Soon everyone was ready to go into the barn for cider and gingerbread. It was during these waiting moments that I first heard the voice of the Lord. His voice was audible and seemed to come from above. His words were simply, "This is the one." I knew it was my Lord! Just how could He care so much that He would speak to me? Once more I was made to realize that God knew about the things that were happening in my life, that He cared, and that this courtship was designed of Him.

I told no one of this revelation, but kept it as a precious secret and pondered it as our relationship grew and developed into a beautiful romance.

After the war years, the manufacturing of cars rose to an all-time high. Every auto dealer had a long waiting list. Paul had placed his name on one of these lists and was impatiently waiting his turn. Several days before Christmas, he was notified that a green Studebaker had arrived and that his name had finally reached the top of the list. He was happy that he no longer needed to borrow the family car for our dates. The neat little Studebaker sported a wrap-around glass window at the back and was equipped with the new convenience of overdrive, which was designed to save money in gas mileage.

Paul's interests and mine were much alike, for we both loved the Lord. We never tired of being together nor ran out of conversation. By spring we realized that our hearts were being strongly knit together by love, and the time between our Sunday evening dates seemed to grow longer and longer as we lived for these hours together.

The previous summer my family had traveled to Illinois to visit my Dad's uncle, Dave Forsythe, who owned a nursery. Daddy was contemplating a new vocation and wanted to investigate some of the advantages of the nursery business. In the winter of 1947 we had sale of our cattle and machinery and purchased several acres of rich loam soil for a house and business along a small creek at the south edge of Greencastle.

It was a real blessing to see Mother and Daddy enjoy their own place and business after so many years of toiling for someone else. Even though the work required him to spend many hours in the nursery, Daddy was always happy, and the fertile meadow soil produced beautiful evergreens and flowering shrubs.

Little advertisement was needed since we lived along a route that was one of the main highways in and out of town, and there was not another nursery for miles around. His business prospered.

That fall Paul and I began to plan for an early spring wedding. We were married on March 5, 1949, and the Lord added His blessing by giving us balmy temperatures equal to a May day. We were married in front of the fireplace in my home, which had been decorated with ferns and candelabra. Carrying an arm bouquet of white roses, I came down the open stairway in my white satin gown trimmed in lace with a long train and a fingertip veil. My sister Annabelle was my maid of honor, and Paul's brother Clarence was his best man. A friend of ours played the traditional wedding music on the piano along with one of our favorite hymns, "Saviour, Like a Shepherd Lead Us." The 60 guests shared our reception in our formal dining room.

Paul and I enjoyed an eight-day honeymoon in Florida's sunshine before returning to Pennsylvania to set up housekeeping.

Chapter 6

A Bit of Heaven

Our first house was the original home of Paul's great-grandparents, Isaac and Susanna Grabill. They pioneered from Lancaster to Franklin County in 1864. Before their arrival to the area, half of the house had burned. They stayed with neighbors until Grandfather Isaac could dig clay, burn bricks, and rebuild the house.

By the year 1875, more bricks had been baked and a permanent barn was erected, one that remains in good condition to this day. Some years later, a second set of buildings were built about half a mile to the east.

This is the farm on which Paul was born and where he spent his 21 years prior to our marriage. It was also here that I discovered that a marriage can be everything God intended it to be when each person gives himself to the other and puts the partner's happiness ahead of his or her own desires.

Our first task was to paint some of the woodwork and hang wallpaper to give our house a fresh, new look. Because we did not have money to hire a professional, we undertook each job that needed done by ourselves. Paul was a hard-working man and not afraid to tackle a new challenge. We learned to live and enjoy our new life together. One of our choicest secrets for a good marriage has been the necessity of always sharing everything, our thoughts, dreams, and hurts, and talk about them.

Early each morning Paul crossed the fields to his parents' farm to milk the cows and work the fields. He came home for lunch and left again, returning when the evening milking and feeding chores were finished. These were long days for me.

At that time women who continued outside public work after their marriage were frowned upon. I quit my secretarial job before our wedding. When boredom became too much for me, I walked over to visit my mother-in-law and sisters-in-law. Elizabeth, Rhoda, Bertha, Naomi, and Dorcas were all still at home, and we had many nice times together.

A woman's natural desire for motherhood combined with those long, lonely days resulted in a July pregnancy. For four long months morning sickness was a 24-hour endurance. My body became thin, for I was unable to digest any food, even with medication. I could not keep up my household duties, and found it necessary to go back to my parents' home for several months. I became so weak, I even needed help to walk. I greatly appreciated my compassionate husband during this time as he traveled the distance each evening to spend the night with me and give me comfort.

In March when wild Canadian geese made their flight northward once more, we talked of the approaching busy farm days. It was a cold spring, and by the first of April, only a few robins had ventured into our area. Yet spring was still in the air; the apricot tree was pushing forth blossoms in full magnificence. All earth seemed to be holding its breath waiting for something special…or perhaps I was only sensing my own anticipation to hold that little life in my arms.

On the morning of April 13, 1950, I awoke early. I immediately knew that the time for my baby's appearance was near. Some think of Friday the thirteenth as a bad omen, but not us! Before the end of the day, I was holding our little seven-pound son Shannon in my arms, thrilled at the lovely black hair and perfectly formed body. We thanked God for His wonderful gift of life to us.

Seven days later Paul took the baby and me from the Waynesboro Hospital to my parents' home. All seemed well that day, but by the next evening I was running a high fever. Dr. Hess came to the house and told me that I would need to return to the hospital.

With medication, I was given permission to wait until morning for admittance. That night the Holy Spirit reminded me of the promise made to the believers in James 5:14-15:

> *Is any sick among you? let him call for the elders of the church; and let them pray over him, anointing him with oil in the name of the Lord: and the prayer of faith shall save the sick, and the Lord shall raise him up; and if he have committed sins, they shall be forgiven him.*

I asked my family to contact the ministers to come for the anointing service, believing that this promise would be mine. I dreaded leaving my baby to Mother's care. Although with a fever of 104.5, I knew I needed a quick touch from the Great Physician.

The elders came to anoint me for healing after the evening church services, and Mother slept on the couch by my bed that night. Several hours passed, and I began to slip into a valley of darkness. I knew this was the valley of death. I seemed to be floating away from the earth. It felt like a weightless drifting. I felt as if I needed to get my mother's promise to care for my baby; however, I could not speak. Not a sound could I force from my lips; my strength ebbed away; and I was forced to relinquish my thoughts and go deeper into the darkness. I did not sense fear or loneliness, just a concern that I did not want to leave my husband and the baby behind. I experienced no realization of time, no feeling of gravity, only a sense of floating through space.

Then out of the darkness I felt two hands softly touch the top of my head, and gently follow down my body until they touched my feet. The touch was awesome! I knew it was Jesus who met me in this dark valley! Strength flooded my complete being as everything turned light. Immediately I was back in my bed. I called out, "Mamma, Jesus came and touched me!" Tears of joy streamed down our faces. My temperature was now normal, and I wanted something to eat. It was midnight, and what a glorious touch I had received!

The next morning we notified Dr. Hess what had happened, that I had been anointed with oil by the elders of the church and was healed. He was a Christian and knew that a miracle had indeed taken place.

I had experienced a new step on my Christian journey, for I had had an actual encounter with the living Christ, a personal, powerful Savior! From the time I was very young, my favorite Scripture had been Romans 12:1-2:

> *I beseech you therefore, brethren, by the mercies of God, that ye present your bodies a living sacrifice, holy, acceptable unto God, which is your reasonable service. And be not conformed to this world: but be ye transformed by the renewing of your mind, that ye may prove what is that good, and acceptable, and perfect, will of God.*

I now knew this was indeed my reasonable service.

Many times when I am asked to perform some service and my flesh is not willing, I remember this covenant and step out in His strength. Truly, "I can do all things through Christ which strengtheneth me" (Phil. 4:13).

The redbrick church at Upton, which we attended, had served my husband's ancestors for many years. When we married, the attendance numbered 33. Anyone willing to work was assigned a task. Paul was elected to serve as Sunday school superintendent, and I was assigned a class of children to teach. We were a congregation of three church houses: Brandts, Shanks, and Upton. We longed to see some growth in our area and prayed that the Lord would use us in some way to make this a reality.

In August 1951, we attended the semi-annual council meeting held at the Brandt house. Among the business was the election of a deacon. The same procedure of election was followed as the calling of a man to the ministry.

The leaders read First Timothy 3:8-13:

> *Likewise must the deacons be grave, not double tongued, not given to much wine, not greedy of filthy lucre; holding the mystery of the faith in a pure conscience. And let these also first be proved; then let them use the office of a deacon, being found blameless. Even so must their wives be*

grave, not slanderers, sober, faithful in all things. Let the deacons be the husbands of one wife, ruling their children and their own houses well. For they that have used the office of a deacon well purchase to themselves a good degree, and great boldness in the faith which is in Christ Jesus.

After each person cast his vote before a visiting District Representative, the call to the office was announced. Brother Jacob Miller, a tall, hefty man with an authoritative voice, announced that three men had been chosen, and with the officials' agreement, it was decided that God would have all three couples installed for service. I can still hear his booming voice call, Edgar and Frances Grace Martin, John and Ruth Grove, and Paul and Betty Jane Negley. We were asked to come forward, and the people extended their blessings to us.

After our year of proving our faithfulness to the work, we were ordained as lifetime deacons with the laying on of hands in a consecration service.

Our new responsibilities were to preach in the absence of a minister, visit the sick, and see that the needs of the poor and widows were met. In addition to this, we were to attend to the business of the Love Feast and communion service and make the annual visit to each of the members to determine if everyone was in unity and willing to function in the work of the church.

After several years our congregation began to grow. Several new families moved to our area, which encouraged us and helped to lighten the work. Because regulations governing the use of tires and gasoline eased up, people were able to visit neighboring congregations for special services.

We could not spend time away from the farm for long vacations; therefore, we took great delight in visiting neighboring churches and fellowshiping with our friends there. One Sunday we visited the Pleasant Hill church where one of our ministers was holding a revival. We were invited home for lunch by Samuel Lehigh, one of the ministers of that congregation. Not knowing his wife had also extended several invitations, 20-some persons came

to the house that day. After I offered my help, Sister Lehigh took
me into her back kitchen. Brother Lehigh proceeded to saw three
large slices from a home-cured ham. I was given a granite pan full
of potatoes to peel. A quart of frozen corn was brought from the
freezer to cook. We also peeled and sliced fresh tomatoes and
opened canned peaches to serve with ginger snaps. After peeling
the potatoes, I was asked to trim and cut the ham into pieces.

I knew there were many people fellowshiping on the porch,
and I wondered just how small I was to make the pieces. I was full
of anxiety about it not being sufficient for the crowd. Finally, I
turned it over to the Lord: "Lord, you multiplied the loaves and
fishes on the hillside many years ago, and I know you can multiply
what we have today." Resting in this thought, I relaxed and took
Sister Lehigh's instructions.

The table was set three times, with plenty for everyone and
food left over. I was overwhelmed to know that God had been in
our midst and had performed this miracle for these precious saints
who were blessing us with their gift of hospitality.

We often wondered, *Did anyone else realize that God had multiplied the food?* Many years later we met one of the other couples who had been present that Sunday. As they were trying to
recall where we had met, they surprised us by saying: "Oh, you
are one of the couples who were at Lehighs the day the food multiplied." How blessed we were to know that others also knew of
this miracle.

The Lehighs have been in heaven with the Lord many years. At
the time of this miracle, this dear couple was in their seventies.
Our fond recollection of that memorable day will linger forever.

Further changes were made on the farm that year as Paul's father decided to revamp the original barn of 1875 for dairying. Two
brown silos and a concrete milk house were built. The interior of
the barn was cleared of stables, feeding troughs, and hay racks.
Concrete floors were poured, and a stanchion system was installed. By the spring of 1953, the herd of dairy cattle was divided
between Paul and his brother. This provided a new challenge in
animal husbandry, and we became more independent and happy.

Soon after this division, my father-in-law suffered a stroke and was no longer able to farm. By early spring Mother Negley bought a small, brick bungalow near Marks, which she often referred to as her "cottage."

The Lord continued to bless our herds and fields as we depended on Him from day to day.

Chapter 7

A Completed Family

By the fall of 1953, I was experiencing another difficult pregnancy. This one confined me to bed for seven long months. Paul's sister Naomi came and stayed with us to take over the household chores. Each day was a lesson of faith, patience, and endurance for each of us.

Rachel Gingrich, a minister's wife from across the fields, often came to visit and always brought me good Christian literature from their Mennonite church library. Many were stories about missionaries. I often wondered if God was trying to tell me something by the books she chose. As the months passed, I began to sense that the child I was carrying would one day be called to serve in the mission field.

Each day I promised the Lord that if He would give me this child, I would be willing to give him or her to the work that He designed. Paul was very patient and helpful; the days of my doctor's checkups meant he needed to carry me to the car and into the doctor's office. Each time I felt stronger and tried to work, I would have to return to bed to keep from miscarrying.

Shannon was now an active little fellow of three, and he enjoyed the long hours on my bed as I read to entertain him. Paul's sister Naomi was a wonderful help during this time, and I am sure she remembers the mountain of pancakes it took at each breakfast to satisfy her big brother's appetite.

Rosanna Marie was born April 26, 1954, a beautiful, six-pound, black-haired darling. We rejoiced that the Lord had brought us through this valley and blessed us with such a lovely daughter.

Like all parents, we had our difficult days of sickness. Both children were susceptible to croup. On many occasions we built a tent with sheets over a rocking chair or their beds along with a vaporizer containing the most potent medication that could be prescribed. We took our turns rocking the children, singing, and praying under the tent. Shannon's favorite hymn was "Sweet Hour of Prayer."

Back home in Greencastle, my parents' business was prospering. Daddy had all the work he could handle alone with his asthmatic condition. The spring and fall plantings and diggings were taking a toll on his health. By evening he was exhausted and his breathing labored. He was only 49. The laborious years of the Great Depression on the farm and the foundary had taken their toll.

Our family shared Thanksgiving dinner at Kenneth and Opal's home. We enjoyed a traditional meal of roast turkey, scalloped oysters, and all the trimmings.

That night Daddy's breathing became unusually labored, and he was rushed to the hospital. About midnight the whole family was called to his bedside. We sought God for his recovery, but it was time for Daddy's homegoing.

Mother stayed with us for several weeks; but since she was only 49, she wanted to maintain her own home even though she knew she would need to give up the business.

At this time none of us owned our own properties, so Mother gave each of us some small plants as she looked ahead, with the hope that as we purchased homes, the shrubbery would be large enough for nice landscaping. In that way we would each have our own memorials.

Later, Mother sold the nursery and home and purchased a large brick house in Chambersburg. She converted it into four apartments and lived in one of them. The Lord blessed her with this investment.

During this year of grief, my brother Richard bought her a gift of oil paints and canvases. From early childhood she possessed artistic ability. Painting proved to be more than therapeutic for her, for in future years she sold many paintings and continued to paint until she was 75 years old.

After a year of being widowed, mother married Wilbur Kline, a deacon and widower from her church. They had many good days together and enjoyed particularly their project with the Knobsville Church of the Brethren. It was a small congregation without a minister in the Tuscarora mountain range. Mother and Wilbur volunteered to serve at this place. New friendships were established, and the church began to grow during their time there. They served that congregation until the district assigned a full-time pastor.

While they served there, a poor family in the congregation had a house fire. Their greatest need was for money to build a chimney. The Lord impressed me to put my compassion into action. One bitter cold, windy day in February, I bundled up the children and drove to Mother Negley's, asking her to babysit while I solicited funds from our Christian friends. She was happy to assist and was the first to give me a donation for the little collection box that I had made.

A builder had been contacted and a price had been submitted for the rebuilding of the chimney. In later years, I learned that God had given me a gift of faith for this venture as I knew in my heart that somehow He would move on persons to give the amount of money needed to build the chimney. I promised the Lord that I would go in faith and not look into the box until my errand was finished.

Grandma had a long day of babysitting, for it was dark by the time I finally pulled into her driveway. Together we opened up the box and found the exact amount of money for the contractor's estimate. Our hearts leaped for joy! The chimney was erected shortly thereafter. One of the daughters of this family was so touched that complete strangers would care enough to help that she became convicted and accepted the Lord as her Savior.

These times of spiritual blessing never seemed to come frequently enough for us. We loved walking in the Spirit and feeling the Lord's leading. When Paul could not accompany me, he supported me with his prayers and encouragement.

We continued to see slow growth in our congregation. Several children were reaching the age of accountability, and a few relatives of families were also added to our number. We attended Sunday morning and evening services and the mid-week Bible studies, but something was still lacking in our lives. What was missing? Why were there weeks and months of spiritual drought? We wanted so much to experience those refreshing times of the Holy Spirit daily.

In the summer of 1956, the trustees decided to remodel the Upton church. The raised benches at the ends were torn out, and the floor of the one-room sanctuary was put on one level. We bought other pews and built a raised pulpit at the south end of the room. The wooden floor of the sanctuary was tiled, and carpet was laid in the aisles. This was a welcomed renovation.

One warm May day, Paul was down in the hollow plowing for corn when one of his sisters came to tell us that Pop was very sick and we were to come immediately. When we arrived at the house, he had already slipped into eternity. Mother Negley had spent four long years caring for Pop since his stroke, and her strength was waning. Because she no longer desired to have the burden of farming decisions, arrangements were made to sell the farms to Paul and his brother Clarence.

Soon after purchasing the farm, we remodeled the house. With these new conveniences, I began to propose to Paul the possibility of trusting God for another child. With the difficulty of my past pregnancies, this matter was earnestly taken before the Lord. In faith we decided to trust Him, and I became pregnant that fall. Things were not as complicated this time, but we still needed the help of his sister Dorcas, who came to live with us for several months.

Katrina Sue was born June 8, 1960, in the Chambersburg Hospital. Paul described her as our precious Indian doll with her mass of black hair that hung down to her eyebrows. She was a doll, captivating everyone's attention.

Paul and I enjoyed the challenges and rewards of parenting as we endeavored to train our children for the Lord. We were thrilled with nature excursions across the fields to gather wild orange poppies and yellow snapdragons as we brought the cows in from the pasture for milking. I have fond memories of those tiny fists presenting me with dandelions and freshly picked violets.

The love and sunshine in the children's smiles erased all the hard moments and sacrifices of motherhood. One particular morning, I recall Shannon came calling me to come out and see an exquisite fog-shrouded cobweb in the branches of the old lilac bush. It was thrilling to see each child become aware of God's handiwork.

Our children loved the outdoors. We had a mulberry tree near the garden gate, with low hanging limbs into which Shannon, Rosanna, and Katrina climbed to eat the sweet black fruit. They often picked the berries which I mixed with sour cherries to make a delicious pie. Another fun place where Katrina often "hid out" was the smoke bush. She spent many hours there reading on hot summer afternoons.

In the winter they made tunnels and igloos in the tightly drifted snowbanks near the house. These banks were not unusual in our area, for strong currents swept down from the Tuscarora mountains and across our level valley. However, sledding, ice skating, and the occasional sleigh ride were the highlights of the winter.

Every autumn we drove through the mountains to view the lovely foliage. We walked along streams and through woods, and we took picnics to the lake or state parks. Winter snows found Paul packing trails for sledding on the inclines, and we often joined our children for the fun or had a neighborhood sledding party.

As the years passed, their education in nature broadened through classes in entomology and flower arranging. These gave way to the greater challenges of growing flowers and sweet corn.

The produce was marketed for money for their bank accounts. However, not every work project was for laying by an amount in their "piggy banks," for we felt it was important to teach our children cooperation with family chores.

Our evening devotions were usually from the Ergiermer's Bible Storybook. We believe there is much truth in the old adage: "The hand that rocks the cradle rules the world."

In January 1962, I was admitted to the hospital for surgery. The day was bitter cold with a real snow blizzard. We took Shannon to Grandma Negley's, while Rosanna stayed with the Ben Shelly family. By the time we reached Grandma Kline's house with Katrina the roads had become treacherous.

I was anticipating a ten-day stay after surgery, but I experienced complications when I developed a staph infection. A lady in our community had recently died from similar surgery and infection. Once again I called for an anointing service. Satan would have liked to had the victory, but I had learned that God's promises could be mine. The Lord heard my cries, and I was delivered by His mighty hand. With each of these valley experiences and God's gracious touch came a greater longing to tell others about the power of God.

The Gayman family, whose farm joined our boundary, were exceptional neighbors. Jacob and Elizabeth were Christians in every sense that the word implies. Early in Elizabeth's married life, she had been stricken with multiple sclerosis. Her continued patience and love demonstrated her great faith as she cheered her friends and relatives. Through the years my respect and love for her only deepened.

As her condition worsened, her husband asked us to farm his place. After six years of this arrangement, Mr. Gayman sold us his farm. The grandfather who had lived at one end of the long, 12-room stone and brick home died. Jacob now felt free to build a new home on the corner of his property where he could more conveniently care for Elizabeth.

This farm was first deeded to William McKenzie in 1774. The original deed, with the King of England's signet stamped in wax, had been drawn up on a fine piece of sheepskin. The intricate handwriting of a quill pen stated that corner posts were marked by oak and hickory grubs and saplings. This tract of land, deeded two years before the signing of the Declaration of Independence, was the large original tract from which the Gayman and Negley farms had been taken.

That year, the day after Thanksgiving, I was enjoying a *Pennsylvania Farmer* magazine, and in the ladies section I found a recipe for a dark, moist fruitcake. This was the beginning of many experiments with baking fruitcakes until I finally perfected a rich, moist cake. The cakes were easy to box and handle in pretty Christmas tins, and many of them were shipped over the country and to servicemen overseas.

My baking stretched from the middle of October into January, or until I could no longer get my seasonal ingredients. I baked for the public for seven years. Eventually I realized I was being caught up in materialism, and I felt guilty for commercializing on the birth of Christ.

During the fall that I began to bake cakes, Paul had a lot of back problems, as many farmers do, from the heavy lifting in hay making, hauling and gathering stones from the fields, preparing for planting, and carrying tons of milk produced through dairying. Paul was hospitalized for a week and sent home in a body cast for several weeks of rest. Paul's rest in the cast brought some relief, but we realized the time had come for us to invest in some labor-saving equipment.

Working with the soil has a way of keeping a farmer dependent on his heavenly Father, for he is constantly aware of weather changes that affect production. The farmer depends not only on the sunshine for growth of crops, but also for the drying of alfalfa for feed. Rain and thunderstorms are needed so the lightning flashes can release nitrogen into the air for the rapid growth of corn and other crops. Even short dry spells are needed to send the roots of corn deep so that they can survive hot summer days and the strong winds of the autumn season.

In 1961 my sister Annabelle suddenly became ill. She had a se-vere headache and her body became rigid. She was taken to the hospital by ambulance and was admitted to an isolation room. Many tests were made in the following weeks; finally the dreaded diagnosis of multiple sclerosis was given. I was grief stricken as now I had to see my only sister go through the same things my dear friend Elizabeth was suffering. How I wished we lived in the days when Jesus had walked on the earth, for I knew He surely would have relieved the suffering of these two sweet women and healed them of this terrible disease.

Chapter 8

Our Thai Daughter

The national organization of 4-H Clubs of America participates in an international exchange of farm youth. These young students spend six months with a family in the United States observing our agricultural methods. In 1965, we were chosen by Pennsylvania State University to host an exchange student from Thailand. Supalak Promtep was a 24-year-old teacher of English in her native country. She was an emissary for her father, who was an affluent leader in his government for their department of agriculture.

Excitement pervaded the atmosphere of our home as we cleaned every nook and cranny of the house and barn in preparation for Supalak's arrival. Would we understand her? Could she communicate with us? Will she want rice at every meal? These were the anxieties that beset our minds as we awaited her arrival. The day finally came and all of our fears were eased as she greeted us with hugs and kisses. She was a vivacious, adorable, little Oriental woman, with so much love and appreciation that she immediately captured our hearts. God gave us a wonderful privilege in allowing us to share in a part of her life.

We were involved in a whirlwind of activity from the beginning, with speaking engagements, dinner parties, and tours of the area. She thrilled at the American farmer's progress. She loved to visit our fruit orchards and pick fruit for herself from the heavily-laden branches. "What are these little purple fruits?" she asked as she gingerly bit into one of the not-so-ripe plums and screwed up her pretty tan face with its sourness. It was appalling to her that apples could be everywhere, even on the ground, when in her country the cost of one apple was fifty cents.

She was so glad "this mamma" cooked rice, for she was so hungry for her country's staple and could not imagine that many Americans did not include it in their diets. While here she had difficulty with her eyes. We took her to an eye specialist who informed her that she needed to get back to her diet of unpolished rice in order for her condition to improve.

Sue, as we called her, was a Buddhist and took her religious life seriously. However, the first day she was with us she took our Bible from the table and said, "Mamma, I have been in America almost six months now and I must know more about Jesus before I return to Thailand; please will you be the one to help me?" She sat down beside me with such a searching countenance which I could not reject or dismiss. Our instructions clearly stated we were not to "indoctrinate" our guest. But it was impossible to turn away from those pleading eyes. I silently prayed for wisdom and a witness that she could grasp in spite of the cultural difference and language barrier. She was asking for help, I reasoned to myself. I was not forcing my beliefs upon her, and she must have her questions answered.

"You must teach me from the very beginning," she urged softly. "I want to know about the ark and the twelve men Jesus chose. What were they to do?" On and on her questions came that day and the next and the next until we had no more days left. She had been in the States five months and shared that time with eight families from Iowa to Pennsylvania. She had attended various churches and gleaned enough information to arouse her interest in Christ.

An old lady in Bedford had given her a well-worn Bible, and she knew from this woman that in it was stored a great treasure. With the flurry of activity, our moments of study were scarce but precious as the Holy Spirit began to open and illuminate her mind. For a farewell gift we presented her with a copy of the Amplified

Bible with the hope that the many adjectives of this version would aid her in its understanding.

With each passing day, we became more endeared to each other, and we dreaded her departure. Sue shed the biggest tears I have seen as she talked of going to her next family. They splashed down across her cheeks like great rain drops. The day before she was to leave, she begged us to hide her in our attic. We sensed this partly came from her desire to know the Lord that had not been fully satisfied and she felt that she may never be placed with another family who would help her. But the Lord had that arranged and placed her with more Christians.

She explained that she understood that Lord Buddha and Lord Jesus were both God's sons; the one for her people and the other for Christians. "I will pray to both of these Gods until I find which one is the true and greatest God," she said. We promised we would continue to write and answer her questions by mail.

Through the months that followed, many lengthy letters of teaching crossed the ocean with the prayer that the Holy Spirit would accompany them with understanding. When she received the answers to one letter, a new question was soon sent; and so the correspondence continued. During this period of time in northern Thailand, many uprisings and communistic infiltrations were taking place. Accounts of robbery and other forms of danger, especially for the educated or wealthy, were relayed to us.

One day upon returning from a business trip to Bangkok, she found everything had been stolen from her room except the two Bibles she had left lying on her bed. She rejoiced that her "precious books" were feared by the robbers. In this incident Sue saw the hand of the Lord and His love for her as she searched out to know the truth of Jesus Christ and Buddha.

Shortly thereafter, a providentially planned illness struck our little brown-skinned daughter when she became critically ill from a kidney infection. Because of her extreme pain and fever, she was flown to Bangkok for the removal of a kidney. She arrived in the city after three days of intense suffering. Soon after being placed in her bed, she was praying and Jesus appeared by her bedside, smiled at her, and disappeared. All pain and fever left her body.

When she wrote she explained, "Mamma, He looked so kind, how I wish I could have heard Him speak a word to me, but He just gave me a loving smile, then He was gone. I knew at once that it was Jesus and that He is the true God. Waves of peace and rest I never knew before came over me, and I went to sleep and slept for many hours."

Three days later the doctors released her as completely healed with no surgery. She returned to her home in Cheingma Province in the northern part of Thailand as a born-again Christian. Over and over she rejoiced in the great mercy of the true God that He had shown her personally, for in this way she came to know that Jesus Christ is God's Son for her people as well.

Supalak longed for Christian fellowship but found little in her country. One Christmas eve she heard a Christian radio program. What a Christmas gift that was to her!

About five years and many letters later, Sue decided to marry. Her friend was a Buddhist school teacher. She wrote and invited us to fly over for the wedding, requesting that if we could not come, she would like us to send a portrait of our family to set in the wedding. Two days before the wedding, she had a heart attack and the ceremony was postponed. We have not heard from her since that time. We believe that it was not in the Lord's plan for her to marry out of her newfound faith, and she was called to her eternal home. In our spirits we know that one day we will be reunited with our precious Thai daughter in the glory world.

Chapter 9

Our Chilean Son

The International Farm Youth Exchange Program was successful in broadening our desire to know more people from around the world and impact our community with this humanitarian vision. The following year our school district organized an American Field Service Chapter to host a foreign exchange student, and we were asked to consider being the host family.

The primary requirement was for the host family to have a child near the same age and grade level in school. Because Shannon satisfied this requirement by being a junior in high school, we filed application with the New York headquarters and waited anxiously to know if we would be accepted. In July we received word that we would be receiving Osvaldo Leyton from Santiago, Chile. He was 18 and would be entering the senior class.

We exchanged pictures and details about our families and began the wait for his arrival in July. We met him at the Harrisburg Bus Terminal on a hot, sultry, July evening. The bus arrived late; and when it pulled in, many weary students scanned the faces of the crowd for their host families. Our family was also filled with anxiety, and with one chorus we all shouted, "There he is!" The thick black hair and eyes from his picture were unmistakable. He was our son for a year! The tired lines of his face spoke of the long trip from his home in Triaco to Santiago, on to New York and to Pennsylvania all within a day. Our greetings were warm but somewhat restrained. *Will he like us?* we wondered.

On the way home we tried to converse but found it quite difficult as his pronunciation of English was very broken, and we knew very few words of his language. For the first few weeks the Spanish-English dictionary was a constant help as we learned to communicate the essentials, and laughed our way through some really funny conversations.

In later years as we visited a Spanish speaking country, I realized what a perplexing time it must have been for "Ozzie," as we nicknamed him. Alone in a new culture, studies in a different language, adjusting to a very different family and routine, and a new education system all created a demanding adventure for an 18-year-old student.

Osvaldo met his challenge bravely. He was studious, with a strong determination to succeed and make the most of this opportunity in America.

A new dimension of love and forbearance was to be demonstrated in our family circle. We each learned to give more of ourselves and to forego many selfish ways as we meshed with a new personality. This set the stage for a tremendous amount of maturity in our family.

Every person should be proud and loyal to his own country. Yet this was a point that required an intricate balance, for our countries had many differences. For Osvaldo the political and economical pursuits of America in Chile left marks of bitterness. Were we truly decent people? This was a question that he needed to personally reckon with and settle in his mind before we could be fully accepted. This image of the past could only be erased with many acts of genuine love and kindness. We all needed to acknowledge that everywhere in the world individuals must share and fellowship on a one-to-one basis for the preservation of peace and tranquility. Only this action will foster brotherly love among nations.

Our religious practices, too, were different from those of his Catholic background, and in this we were scrutinized carefully. He had little good for those who upheld religion in his life. The only two priests he knew had been unfaithful to their vows of celibacy. They had been implicated in the lives of the nuns at the boarding school Osvaldo attended. This cast a shadow on the reality of religion and the necessity of it in his life.

Living under his intelligent and watchful eye was a great challenge for us in exercising the fruit of the Spirit. It was important that no hypocrisy be seen in our spiritual lives as he judged our sincerity. With patience, we awaited his genuine acceptance of our love.

Seven months later during our spring evangelistic services, Katrina felt the call of the Lord upon her life. Our evangelist, Samuel Castle, was a quiet, anointed speaker who addressed the importance of committing one's life to Christ. Osvaldo was noticeably moved with her decision and spent most of the day quietly in his bedroom.

The country atmosphere provided little for Osvaldo to find to fill up his time. His studious mind was constantly reaching for more knowledge. If there was not a new book available, he would study the encyclopedia. His ultimate dream in life was to be a medical doctor, and we felt sure with his brilliant mind and determination that one day in the future this would become a reality.

Osvaldo spent his carefree moments with Shannon's guitar, strumming and singing his favorite Spanish songs. This seemed to soothe some periods of homesickness, as he thought of his mamita and sister Ximena. He missed his brother Ramon and the trips when they drove their thousands of sheep and goats up the slopes to graze in new areas of the Andes Mountains. His melancholy expressions were visibly noticed as he recalled the times he spent with the cowboys and his grandfather's beautiful horses as they herded the flocks high into the snow-covered passes toward fresher pastures near the border of Argentina. "Ramon is a good cook," he said. "Nothing is as good as his roast lamb made on an open fire in the pasture after a long ride with the sheep."

One cold winter morning in February, Osvaldo came down for breakfast looking quite miserable. When I looked at him, I knew he was indeed sick and had the evidence to prove it. To him it was the "horror of all horrors," as I handed him a mirror for him to see the red splotches of a full-blown case of chicken pox. The worst thing for Osvaldo was to hear from the doctor that he must not study or use his eyes much for several days. For him this was a terrible restriction, and he still considers this his worst experience in America.

Osvaldo was an excellent first student for the exchange program for our school. He impressed both his peers and the faculty. He spoke at many organizational meetings for men's clubs and civic groups and left our school and community with a good understanding of Chile. Some years later a student from James Buchanan was sent to Santiago for a year through the same program. Twenty-five years later this program continues to be fruitful in fostering international relationships in our community.

We dearly loved Osvaldo and accepted him as a son in our family. The year went by quickly, and we hated to see him leave. The day before his departure, he took an urgent telephone message that there was a barn fire nearby. He came running to us with the message, and we looked across the fields to see flames rising from Clarence's barn. Osvaldo stayed home with the girls, while Paul and I jumped in the truck and headed over to help. I ran to the house and helped my sister-in-law to summon several fire companies. Somehow we dashed into the milk house, just under the flames, and brought out the milker machines, buckets, and other small equipment.

Anxious time, which seemed to be hours, passed and I knew that Paul and Clarence would be fighting the fire at some strategic point near the walkway in an effort to save the second barn. When the firemen arrived, they considered it unsafe to go into this passage; but I saw Paul take the hose from them and go in, which made others willing to follow at this blocking point.

Seven fire companies arrived with their equipment, and men from everywhere came running to assist. The dense smoke rose from the mow of burning hay, and flames and sparks savagely licked upward as the roof caved in on the tons of hay from the summer's harvest. The trees in the yard yielded their green leaves to the scorching heat as the inferno raged on. With a small change of wind, surely the house would go too. For a time, we women questioned whether we should start to carry things from the house. How helpless we felt! What could we do? We prayed for the safety of the men and tried to comfort the children as they stood by with tears of fright streaming down their faces.

In one of those low moments as I stood and beheld the power and destruction of fire, I felt a gentle arm slip around my shoulder, and I looked up to see the compassion and tenderness of Jesus in the eyes of a teenage boy from the community. Marvin Hissong had no words, but his gentle expression of sympathy spoke volumes to sustain me and gave me new courage to believe for the safety of my husband and the other men as the fire roared on in its fury.

The brave men fought the fire for many hot hours until it was finally under control. Everyone seemed to have a heart; women came with cold drinks and sandwiches to refresh the firemen. Neighbors came with forks and shovels for the long and difficult task of cleaning out the hot, steaming, unconsumed water-logged hay from the remaining salvageable structure. Others donated trucks to haul the waste away and scatter it over the fields. On into the late evening they worked, their faces and hands black from the dirt and smoking debris. We will never forget the willing, generous hearts of our many friends and neighbors.

That night as we returned from the fire, Osvaldo said, "Mamma, you don't need to worry about my packing, for I have everything ready." The next day we drove him to York where he was to meet the bus that would take the students to the New England states. Each of the young people was to visit with several other families before returning to their homelands. Osvaldo was a stoic young fellow, and we knew he would be embarrassed with any demonstration of emotion in our farewells. Everyone put on a best front as we gave Osvaldo our embraces, a quick kiss, turned our backs, and walked away. When we reached the car and were out of sight, a flood of tears broke uncontrollably down my face. I had really learned to love that boy, and we doubted that we would ever see him again.

Several days later he surprised us with a call from Connecticut. He wanted to express his gratitude and to say that now he understood our love was truly genuine. He also wanted us to know how he felt about us. We praise the Lord that our lives had effectively exemplified the love of Jesus.

Twelve years and many letters had come and gone since Osvaldo's time with us until one night we received a call from Miami. It was Dr. Osvaldo Leyton, who was now a surgeon at one of the hospitals in Santiago. He had come to the States for a medical convention and would be coming to visit us in a few days. With great excitement and joy, we met him at the Harrisburg airport a few days later. As I saw him coming up the corridor, I could not restrain my emotions as I ran to greet him. He was no longer our young teenager; he was now a mature young man. Neither was he embarrassed to return our love as we lovingly embraced after the years of separation.

He shared with us that he had found the lady he wanted to marry. Maria Euguenia was a young nurse who worked at his hospital. If his marriage proposal was accepted, he would be bringing her to our home and Miami the next year during their wedding trip.

The following October we met him and Maria Euguenia at the Hagerstown airport within 24 hours of the ceremony. She is a delightful, petite, sweet, Spanish lady, who compliments Osvaldo's life perfectly.

Now we thought of them as a family and began to dream of the day we might have the opportunity to visit in their home and see the children who may be added to their union. We longed to know Mamita, Ximena, and Ramon, to go to Triaco and see Grandfather Leyton's farm, to see the sheep and goats on the Andes Mountains, to taste the food Osvaldo had spoken of, and to see the ports of Chile's Pacific coastline. One day, yes, perhaps one day this would become a reality.

Chapter 10

I've Heard the Voice of God

Time moved on, and the Lord's blessings surrounded us as we watched our children move from one stage of maturity to the next. Shannon had now been dating a lovely girl for about a year. Marian Frey was the daughter of one of our ministers. Her parents, Kenneth and Anna Mary Frey, were close friends of ours; consequently, we knew Marian well and were pleased with the deepening relationship between them.

When they announced their plans to be married in May, it was no surprise to us. We were contemplating the necessity of an expansion of our farming operation if they chose to stay on with the business. Changes would be essential to provide a two-family income.

During the fall before the wedding, a large loafing barn was erected, another silo was built, and mechanical feeding and other new time-saving ideas were incorporated at the cost of $30,000. Financially, things looked good and we were comfortable.

The county agent desiring to initiate new ideas in farm management had chosen our farm as one of three in the county that year for the annual winter farm tour. Paul had devised some unique ideas of his own by joining the new barn to the older one to save labor in feed handling.

Paul and Shannon enjoyed working with the new equipment, and all went well until August of the following year when we learned the Lord had other plans for our lives. Romans 11:33 best describes the new truth we were about to learn: "O the depth of the riches both of the wisdom and knowledge of God! how unsearchable are His judgments, and His ways past finding out!"

It was sweet corn harvesting time, and I was preparing the delicious Iochief corn for the freezer. Paul and Shannon had stored 450 bales of alfalfa in the barn that day. It was one of those hot, muggy days when you felt you needed a pusher to keep moving. About six o'clock Paul came to the house. I saw at once he was pale and that something was wrong. "I am going in to see the doctor; I'm not feeling well," he said. The doctor was concerned that he might have had a slight heart attack and ordered two weeks of complete bed rest.

While in prayer the following day, I heard the voice of God. *"There are changes coming in your life,"* He said. I was frightened. What changes could He mean? Was something to happen to Paul that I would be widowed and need to raise the children alone? After pondering this message for some time, I found strength in knowing that Jesus knew and cared about me and was preparing me for whatever was ahead or He would not have spoken to me in this manner. It was at this time that our family adopted the Lord's assurance found in Romans: "And we know that all things work together for good to them that love God, to them who are the called according to His purpose" (Rom. 8:28). As the days passed the Holy Spirit joined the heavenly message with this Scripture and brought peace to my heart.

When our elder minister inquired about Paul's condition the following Sunday, I told him of hearing the voice of God. He said that someday we would understand what the message meant, but for now we should just walk in faith.

Paul called for the elders to come to anoint him for healing, but nothing changed physically. Two weeks later when Paul returned to the doctor, an enlarged lymph gland was found. This was removed and a biopsy was made at the local hospital. A Harrisburg specialist was called in, who provided the diagnosis of sarcoidosis of the lungs. They explained little about the disease, but we realized that it was serious.

After a night of fitful sleep, I arose early to go to the barn to help with the milking. But before going out I pulled out our medical book, hoping to find out more about the disease. A sketch was given of a sarcoid-diseased lung, with the accompanying definition: "A rare disease of unknown cause, some patients appear chronically ill, a disease of remissions and exacerbations. Advanced stages of infected lungs bring swelling that shrinks the heart, with blood and puss emitted by coughing in advanced cases. To date no means of treatment has been found."

The blow was heavy and crushing as I dropped my head in despair. When Shannon entered the room, I wondered, *How can I spare one so young from the hard facts?* But I knew in my heart there was no way possible, for on his young shoulders would fall the weight and responsibility of the farming operation.

We went to the barn that morning and worked in silence. My mind spun and tears spilled out. Then the Holy Spirit came with this comforting Scripture: "...all things work together for good to them that love God, to them who are the called according to His purpose."

Several days later Paul was discharged from the hospital and given two kinds of medication with the hope they would help in slowing the progression of the disease and make his breathing easier.

Through the months ahead, there were good days and bad days. I had surgery in the summer and was unable to do much work for several months. This left the children with much of the garden work.

I had been on heart medication for several years at this time; and with the extra work and anxiety of my husband's illness, I began to feel exhausted before I had accomplished many of my daily chores. I experienced numbness in my arms and hands, and the doctor bills were becoming immense, not to mention the money that was being spent for our medications. The pressures of two sick parents weighed heavily upon the children's emotions and security, as they wondered what would be the next turn of events.

That summer Shannon developed allergic reactions to hay dust. It was like drawing straws between him and his dad to see who could best stand the mowing of the hay. We felt as if great evil forces were coming against us as we struggled through that summer.

One evening when Katrina was trying to push a bale of hay from the upper barn floor down to the cows, she fell through the hay hole and landed in the cow trough. We carried her into the house. She suffered a light concussion but was not seriously injured.

Soon after this the doctor found that my problem was not my heart, but an inactive thyroid. The new medication did wonders for me. I praised the Lord that at last I could do my part of the chores and had more stamina to cope with all the problems of our family.

However, the battle with sickness continued as Katrina began a series of days out of school. She had no appetite and the skin was peeling from the tips of her fingers. We learned that she had a vitamin deficiency and mononucleosis. By spring, Rosanna contracted mononucleosis as well.

Some persons questioned if we were living right—had we committed some sin or perhaps had the sins of our ancestors been passed on to us? Even though these people meant well, we began to identify with Job and the admonitions given to him by his friends.

Mental anxiety and exhaustion filled each day. Many nights' sleep came to me with great difficulty. We knew God permitted Job's affliction as a test of his faithfulness and righteous living, as he lost his health, family, and property. Could we withstand the possibility of a loss of that magnitude? Would I be able to withstand such tactics of satan, especially the loss of my husband? For comfort, I recalled Job's words from the midst of his great calamity. His words were: "...the Lord gave, and the Lord hath taken away; blessed be the name of the Lord" (Job 1:21). Scripture also says, "In all this Job sinned not, nor charged God foolishly" (Job

1:22). As Paul and I shared our anguish, we reasoned that only God could have brought Job through this test and that should our testing be as severe as Job's, God's divine plan would still be one of victory.

Spring held some new joys and excitement for our family as the wedding bells rang for Shannon and Marian on May 10, 1970. It was a simple but lovely ceremony conducted by her father with approximately 150 guests. After a trip to the New England states, they moved into the newly-decorated stone end of the Gayman homestead.

Marian came from a dairy farm background and willingly assisted Shannon with the milking chores. Later in the summer, they encouraged us to take a few days vacation with the Carl Longeneckers at a summer cottage in the mountains of northern Pennsylvania. Carl, his son Kenny, and our girls loved climbing the mountain just back of the cottage, playing games, and wading in the stream nearby.

Our pleasure was found in things that required less energy, for Paul was getting very short of breath and needed a lot of rest.

At the cottage we awakened to the call of dozens of blue jays as they came for their breakfast of shelled corn placed on the picnic table. During the hours of dawn and dusk, herds of deer cautiously approached the old apple trees that graced the carefully tended acres below the white cottage. They nibbled contentedly at the fallen harvest apples.

We cherished every moment. It was like a bit of heaven to be away from the work and enjoy the bliss of this mountain retreat. Although we never expressed it verbally, we all wondered if this would be our last vacation together. However, the Lord reminded us once more that all things were working together for our good. So step by step, we faced each new day with faith in our God.

The next month when Paul went for his periodical chest x-ray, I also went to see the gynecologist. I was aware that I was having some kind of internal problem. At this appointment the doctor discovered a tumor or growth in my pelvic area. I was scheduled for surgery in ten days. The following afternoon Paul's surgeon called to say his x-rays showed a great change, and they wanted him to be admitted immediately.

A bronchial examination was peformed to determine if there was a tumor to which they could attribute the rapid progression of the disease. His lungs had become greatly enlarged, his heart was shrinking in size, and his breath was becoming increasingly unpleasant. The doctors said nothing could be done, but they prescribed two more kinds of medicine to make him more comfortable.

It was during this time in the hospital that I went into the hospital chapel to pray. I was so burdened and distressed that I thought I would break beneath the load. I stood wearily at the altar a moment before sinking onto the front pew in the dimly lit room. I could not form words to present my petition, but my spirit groaned within me. I felt like the children in Exodus 2:23b-24:

> *The children of Israel sighed by reason of the bondage, and they cried, and their cry came up unto God by reason of the bondage. And God heard their groaning, and God remembered His covenant with Abraham, with Isaac, and with Jacob.*

In Isaiah 65:24, we read, "And it shall come to pass, that before they call, I will answer; and while they are yet speaking, I will hear." I was soon to learn that God had heard my groanings.

About five minutes after I returned to Paul's room a strange woman entered. She approached with a confident air of knowing where she was going, but I was sure I had never seen her before. "I don't believe I know you," I said.

She gave us her name and remarked, "Your husband is very sick, isn't he?"

"Yes," I replied, and then she reached out her hand in authority and laid it on his head and began to pray. Power flowed from her every word! In her prayer she spoke in some strange language we could not understand. Her prayer of about 60 seconds was short, powerful, and to the point. She turned to give me a farewell greeting; and as she extended her hand to touch me, she stopped abruptly. She exclaimed, "Lord, this woman needs healing too." Then my head received the masterful treatment of her prayer and she was gone.

We were like the onlookers of Jesus' day as they beheld the power of Christ, for we were astonished and amazed. Our minds were full of questions: How did this stranger know about us, and who had sent her to the hospital? What was the strange language in the middle of her prayer? Could it have been the Pentecostal tongues we had read about in the Book of Acts? How did the lady know that I also had a problem when she touched me? Could the Holy Spirit reveal something like this to one of His children? We kept all these unusual happenings and pondered these questions in our hearts.

The day for my admittance to the hospital arrived. However, after the stranger's visit, I faced the ordeal with a new hope and assurance that could not be explained. After various tests, the surgeons advised me to wait longer for the surgery, for they discovered the growth was actually a mass of adhesions from former surgery. More surgery would no doubt complicate the problem. God was delaying things for His glory and my benefit, bless His holy name.

Shortly thereafter, our family physician called me to his office for a consultation concerning Paul's condition. He took the medical book from the shelf and sympathetically explained the disease and suggested it would be to my husband's benefit to get away from the work and responsibility of the farms. For several days I was not sure how or if I should confront him with this news. But within myself I knew the time must come sooner or later for him to know. Further delay would accomplish nothing.

That Sunday evening, after the work was finished, we took a stroll out over the hill between the two farms. Hand in hand we stood in silence on top of the knoll. With grateful hearts we gazed across the acres of land and all the Lord had blessed us with during our 22 years together at this place. As we watched the two herds of grazing cattle, Paul slipped his arm about my waist and prayerfully whispered, "The earth is the Lord's and the fullness thereof, the cattle on a thousand hills are Thine, and, Lord, we too, are Yours. Anything You wish to do with us will be what we want, whether it is life or death." We both knew that only the Lord could help us make this surrender and that He would be with us as we made our next steps.

Some days later a dear friend sent us a postcard with the following poem that has meant so much to us, and we would like to share it with our readers.

Step by Step

He does not lead me year by year
Nor even day by day.
But step by step my path unfolds;
My Lord directs my way.

Tomorrow's plans I do not know,
I only know this minute:
But He will say, "This is the way,
By faith now walk ye in it."

And I am glad that it is so,
Today's enough to bear:
And when tomorrow comes, His grace
Shall far exceed its care.

What need to worry then, or fret?
The God who gave His Son:
Holds all my moments in His hand,
And gives them, one by one.

Barbara C. Ryberg

Chapter 11

The Stone Bungalow

One fall evening Paul sat down with the evening paper to look over real estate advertisements. We had decided that we would like to locate somewhere near St. Thomas. We prayed that if it was the Lord's will for us to move to this village, He would help us find a small house there. As Paul scanned the real estate ads, he said, "Here is a brown mountain stone bungalow east of St. Thomas with an adjoining stone garage, one acre of ground on a wooded lot." It sounded like what we were looking for.

We contacted the agent and she drove us out to see the house. We knew at once that this was God's provision. I was intrigued with the unique details of the house, for many of them were the things I had dreamed of in my girlhood days. Plans were made for a settlement date, with possession by December 1, 1971.

When I shared with Mother that we had purchased a house and informed her that it was the home of John Divelbiss, a former building contractor, she recalled something very significant. Mr. Divelbiss had bought the largest order of nursery stock my father had ever sold. This is a fantastic example of how God knows the intimate desires of His children. I previously wrote of Mother giving each of us seedlings at the time of Daddy's death as a memorial. My trees and flowering bushes were too large to transplant after the many years on the farm, but now the Lord had provided us with a home where there were many more pieces from our father's nursery than we had previously owned. There were special hybrid rhododendron, azaleas, a row of floribunda roses, with Daddy's favorite blue mist bush and towering blue spruce at the back kitchen door. A long row of 31 arborvitae lined the side of the lawn near a little workshop. I remember that the man came to the nursery to pick up his order, and Daddy remarked that he gave him an extra tree since he probably would have at least one that would fail to grow. At my first opportunity I ran to the back of the lawn to count. Sure enough, they had all grown, all 31 of them were there! God had blessed them all. Hallelujah!

Once again we had something unusual to add to our growing list of things we were pondering. God surely knew all about the happenings in our life. We know the Bible says He will never leave or forsake us (see Heb. 13:5), but the thought of His caring so intimately for tiny details was far beyond our comprehension.

The next three months were spent cleaning the attic at the farm house, packing, and making the necessary preparations for moving to our new home. The arduous tasks of cleaning and repairing machinery and grooming cattle were mountainous ones for which a constant flow of neighbors, friends, and relatives volunteered. As the sale day neared, Paul was becoming more and more exhausted from the strain and responsibility of preparation.

After discussing what I should do with our finances for the future to provide for the children, we had our attorney draw up our will. Paul instructed me what to do with insurances and other business transactions that would need to be taken care of in the future. Our burial lot and major funeral arrangements were discussed. At this time of his illness, he needed a foam wedge and three pillows in order to sleep so that he could be elevated for breathing.

As the days passed, I pleaded with the Lord to allow Paul to be with us until the sale day was over, for I could not recommend cows concerning production, the sire used in breeding, or the horsepower or condition of tractors and machinery. This information was important to secure a fair price for the equipment and dairy herd.

Moving early in December gave us the additional time to concentrate on the sale preparations again. We prayed for a clear, cold day with frozen ground for parking; and with the windy, cold temperatures this was swiftly coming to pass.

The day before the sale several ladies came to help me prepare a meal for the 18 men who came to build electric fences and bring the frisky heifers from one farm to the other. After lunch another 15 or more men arrived. Some men groomed the cattle, while others parked machinery in long lines in the field near the barn.

About two o'clock in the afternoon, a group of men went to drive the heifers from the other farm to the loafing barn where the sale was to be held. The excitement of many strangers, plus the crisp air after weeks of winter housing invigorated the heifers. Up went their heads, and with tails flying high, fences were broken as if they were made of thread. The cattle scattered across the field in every direction.

In Paul's desire to help in the escapade, the excitement became too much for him. He headed toward the barnyard. I looked out to see him clinging to the fence for support. I hurried to him, and as I got there his legs were buckling under him. The men hauled him into the house in a pickup. I called the doctor, who was now our neighbor at the new house, and he advised me to bring him up immediately. Dr. Simmers helped me to get him into the house and to bed and gave him a shot to put him to sleep. Many wondered if he would make it through the night.

Our Lord had helped us again; and by morning, after much persuasion, the doctor consented to my taking him over to the farm, with strict admonition to be out only a few minutes at a time. He needed the support of my arm and a cane; he sat on the wagon as the small tools and items were auctioned off. We made a place for him to rest in the house, where he was available for Shannon when he needed advice.

The enormous crowd assembled from far and near. We had to turn our backs on many of our gathered treasured and earthly possessions. I believe the relinquishing of some of our choicest cows and heifers was the most difficult sacrifice.

By ten o'clock that night, all but a few cattle and most of the machinery had left the premises. We felt tremendous relief as we dropped our money bag in the bank's night depository on the way home. We fell wearily into bed with hearts full of gratitude to the Lord for seeing us through this ordeal.

We rested for several weeks. During this time of quietness, we experienced an unexplainable inner peace. It was like a quiet inner calm in the presence of the Lord.

I want to record a letter written in November by Rosanna to her friend, Janet Brubaker, a minister's daughter in Lancaster County, Pennsylvania.

> Dear Janet:
>
> I've been wanting to write for several weeks. I wish so much we could sit down and talk. So many things have been happening around here, I feel as if I can't put it all on paper.
>
> The biggest thing, Daddy and Mother have decided to sell the farms. Daddy's brother Clarence is going to buy them for his sons. We bought a little stone house in St. Thomas. It sits on a hill surrounded by trees. I am really happy we have a nice place to go, because it's really going to be hard to leave here. But after all, your health and life are the most important.
>
> I heard about your father's back healing. It is wonderful and I am sure you can't get done praising the Lord.
>
> We can feel the presence of God in these past weeks. Perhaps God has some other work for my parents. Everyone around here was shocked that we are selling out. Some of them don't understand and say such strange things, and this isn't very encouraging to Daddy. I am sure you understand; it was probably the same when your parents had to change because of your dad's affliction.
>
> School is going good and we hope to see you at the Spring Youth Conference.
>
> > Love,
> > Rosanna

With the workload off our shoulders, we lived one day and one step at a time and accepted each day as a gift from the Lord.

Chapter 12

Shekinah Glory

March 5, 1972 was our twenty-third wedding anniversary, but it also proved to be a day of new beginnings. This was the first day Paul was strong enough to attend the morning worship service following his January setback. At the close of the service an announcement was made to hold a chain day of prayer for Paul's healing.

At the exact moment of the announcement, Paul, Rosanna, and I heard the Holy Spirit instruct us to fast. We marveled as we shared together on the way home that we had all been admonished to do so. We had never before seen the importance of fasting in seeking a blessing. However, the command was authoritative and precise; and we certainly wanted to be obedient.

The day of prayer was set for Tuesday. This meant a two-day abstinence from food. Katrina joined us even though she was only 11, for she certainly wanted to see her daddy blessed. We drank water and took a cup of hot tea in the evening. We found the fast was not difficult since it was ordered by the Lord, and we were in sincere prayer for God's ultimate blessing. We were deeply humbled that so many friends cared enough to intercede with us for a miracle.

The next Sunday at church I asked for a moment to thank the congregation for their intercession even though Paul had not experienced a healing. We were experiencing the presence and peace of Jesus in a most remarkable way. However, we did not lose faith that a miracle was still a possibility, but faced each day knowing if life or death was our portion, He would be with us.

At the beginning of April, Shannon came to dig up a 12 by 20 foot plot of lawn for my garden. It was a real trial for my husband to watch me cultivate and plant the plot. But with each little task, he experienced a setback. His energy and strength were diminishing. The doctor advised us to purchase a hospital bed to provide him with a better sleeping position. When the bed arrived, he asked us not to set it up for a little while longer but to store it in the workshop.

The weekend for the annual youth conference was near, and we sent an invitation to Elmer Brubaker's children, Mike and Janet, to spend the weekend with us. We invited their parents to have lunch with us on Sunday. They exuberantly accepted the invitation over the telephone. We learned later after receiving Rosanna's letter that they had been fasting for Paul each Thursday, praying that if they could be a blessing to us that God would bring us together in His time.

After lunch that day of April 23, 1972, the Brubakers witnessed to us their experience of healing and the great things of the Lord that they were learning about. When all at once a strange thing happened to me...I knew...*I knew*! I asked, "Elmer, did you know God sent you to us for a special purpose?" I later learned that at that moment the Holy Spirit had given me a word of knowledge as listed among the spiritual gifts for the church's edification in First Corinthians 12.

> *For to one is given by the Spirit the word of wisdom; to another the word of knowledge by the same Spirit* (1 Corinthians 12:8).

Tears began to stream down the minister's face. "I thought so," he said. "Let us go to prayer, for the Lord is with us."

As we knelt in the middle of our living room, he laid his hands on Paul's head and began a simple prayer. After praying a while, he stopped and asked Paul if he had anything to confess that would hinder his healing. My husband quickly acknowledged a bitterness that had evolved from a misunderstanding in church work that he had not been able to overcome. Matthew 18:15 tells us, "...if thy brother shall trespass against thee, go and tell him his fault between thee and him alone...."

Paul did not want to hurt the person and admit being offended, so he had tried to forgive and forget. We believe without this confession he would have hindered the working power of Christ for his healing that day. Satan has his clever devices. Although many of them seem small, they are effective weapons that will destroy the very life and soul of the believer.

The Brethren minister continued his prayer for only a moment until Paul felt a manifestation of the healing power of Jesus go through his chest. He describes it as a sweet, cool feeling flowing through his lungs, and his breathing came naturally. What a mighty God we serve!

We wept with joy and praised God as the room filled with a brilliant, warm light, which we recognized as the Shekinah Glory of the presence of God. The powerful, magnificent glow lasted only a few moments and is beyond any description in my vocabulary. Because I believe that the Lord confirms the miraculous with His written word, I share this Scripture.

...the light of the sun shall be sevenfold, as the light of seven days, in the day that the Lord bindeth up the breach of His people, and healeth the stroke of their wound (Isaiah 30:26b).

While yet on our knees, I cried, "Dear Lord, take the rest of our life and give us strength to serve you." This was our ultimate surrender and the prerequisite for the second blessing experience.

Brother Brubaker laid his hands on our heads and asked the Lord to bless us with His baptism of the Holy Spirit. We were enraptured with the presence of Jesus—so much so that the words of his prayer made little penetration into our thinking. Immediately my thoughts turned to my sister. Oh, if Jesus would heal her, I would be so thankful. Again I heard His voice, *"Annabelle is next."* No one else heard the voice. I wondered if we should take the minister to her house. But as we arose from prayer and realized the lateness of the hour, Elmer stated that they must be getting back to Lancaster. So I thought that perhaps he could come to pray with her another time.

That evening as we attended the evening service, Paul sang with no shortness of breath for the first time in three years. We sang and then we cried for joy; it was just so wonderful! How could we contain or fathom the strange events of these last few hours!

At the conclusion of the service, our niece Linda was the first to notice the difference in our countenance and came to inquire what had happened. She had been praying for Paul for more than a year, along with John and Reba Hershey, a couple who had opened their home to her during her nursing training. She was elated with God's blessing to us. Outside the church we shared with Shannon and Marian the strange happenings of the afternoon. It seemed as if we were in a state of shock and could hardly realize what all had happened to us.

When Paul was ready to go to bed, he removed the foam wedge and two of the three pillows and laid down to sleep. We both slept like babies every night for weeks. There were no dreams, no disturbances, just perfect rest. It was heavenly!

The next day brought another blessing as Marian gave birth to Marvin Eugene, our first grandchild. How could our family contain the joy of the events of just these two days!

This powerful presence of the Spirit of God made us alive, invigorated, and overflowing with His love. We were burning with a passion to be about whatever He had empowered us to do.

About a week later, Paul kept his established appointment with Dr. Dovey, our family physician. He was overwhelmed that Paul had been healed by the power of God. He said, "Paul, I did all I knew to do for you."

The day of his healing had been so profound and the manifestation of healing had restored his breathing so completely that Paul stopped all his medication that day. When the doctor asked him about the medication and learned that he had stopped all at once, he remarked, "You have had two miracles, for you must gradually go off the medicine you were taking!" Since that time lung x-rays have been taken at least three times for occupational examinations. There are no visible scars on the lungs, and his heart is normal in size.

Prior to this event we had received no teaching on the baptism of the Holy Spirit. It was a foreign term. Satan had a veil over our eyes, and our minds were not illuminated to this truth. After the minister's prayer for us to receive the baptism of the Holy Spirit, that veil was taken away. As we read from the Book of Acts, which is the apostolic commission for the establishing and equipping of the saints to be the extension of Christ's Church today, this truth became clear. This was Jesus' intent for the 120 persons He instructed to go to Jerusalem and wait for the promise of the Father.

For John truly baptized with water; but ye shall be baptized with the Holy Ghost not many days hence. ... But ye shall receive power, after that the Holy Ghost is come upon you: and ye shall be witnesses unto Me both in Jerusalem, and in all Judea, and in Samaria, and unto the uttermost part of the earth (Acts 1:5,8).

The answer to our praying to be more effective in God's service had been answered. So this was the "Second Blessing" experience! Acts 2:39 states, "For the promise is unto you, and to your children, and to all that are afar off, even as many as the Lord our God shall call."

We had struggled so many years to serve the Lord without His power. We all need a personal Pentecost—an encounter with Jesus Christ who is the Baptizer with the Holy Ghost.

And John bare record, saying, I saw the Spirit descending from heaven like a dove, and it abode upon Him [Jesus]. And I knew Him not: but He that sent me to baptize with water, the same said unto me, Upon whom thou shalt see the Spirit descending, and remaining on Him, the same is He which baptizeth with the Holy Ghost (John 1:32-33).

So many lost opportunities were long gone. Yet there was no time for remorse. We needed to put our hands to the plow and press on.

The first plans for Pentecost were given by the teaching of God to Moses in Leviticus 23:15-22. Moses commanded the people to observe all the feasts of Jehovah. There were seven religious festivals to be celebrated every year. The first was the Passover feast, which brought into view redemption and future blessing. The second was the feast of Unleavened Bread, which looked forward to communion with Christ and a holy walk. The feast of Firstfruits foreshadowed Christ's resurrection and those who would be resurrected at His coming. The feast of Pentecost referred to the coming of the Holy Spirit. The feast of Trumpets spoke of the regathering of Israel. And the Day of Atonement was to look forward to the time of Israel's repentance after her time of regathering and when Christ the Messiah will set up His Kingdom. The seventh feast was the feast of Tabernacles. This feast looked forward to the time of restoration, not for Israel alone, but for all nations.

In Scripture the number seven stands for perfection. Every seventh year was a Sabbatical year. After seven Sabbatical years came a fiftieth year known as the year of Jubilee. In essence, this was a year of renewal. During this Jubilee year any unpaid debts were forgiven and slaves were set free. This was a year of great celebration.

Following this timetable, the Pentecost of Acts 2 was on the fiftieth day after the Passover. In similar fashion, the Lord ordained to set us free from the bondage of affliction and pour out His Spirit baptism upon us in accordance with this same biblical pattern. We received our blessing on the fiftieth day following the chain day of prayer and intercession by our friends at church. God has an awesome timetable! This was our Jubilee, a time for celebration, a time of new beginnings.

As the days unfolded into months and into years, we have learned the meaning of the these words in John's first epistle:

> *But the anointing which ye have received of Him abideth in*
> *you, and ye need not that any man teach you: but as the*

same anointing teacheth you of all things, and is truth, and is no lie, and even as it hath taught you, ye shall abide in Him (1 John 2:27).

The Word of God became fresh and understandable. It was no longer a history of other people's lives, but we realized it was His love letter and instruction for us. The promises of the Bible were ours, and the gift of faith made it possible to expect great things from the Lord as the Holy Spirit taught us to go forth in Jesus' name with His power and anointing. God's Word encouraged us in John 15:16:

Ye have not chosen Me, but I have chosen you, and ordained you, that ye should go and bring forth fruit, and that your fruit should remain: that whatsoever ye shall ask of the Father in My name, He may give it you."

The day after Paul's healing, we both felt the prompting of the Spirit to talk to some friends who had never made a commitment to Christ. Conviction fell heavily upon them as we witnessed of God's grace and blessing to us. Later that afternoon Paul testified about his healing to a business associate, who was living in adultery but professed to be living for Christ. He attended church regularly and participated in the church's administration. As Paul shared, the man began to tremble. He fell under great conviction of his sin even though nothing was mentioned about his life of hypocrisy.

With each time of witnessing, Paul's strength grew. That afternoon while shopping in a local supermarket, he felt compelled to raise his arms and stretch. To avoid embarrassment for this unusual behavior, he stood behind some shelves and raised his arms heavenward as he stretched. For days he felt compelled to stretch. We look back on this as the unique way the Lord chose to teach us to praise Him. "Let my prayer be set forth before Thee as incense; and the lifting up of my hands as the evening sacrifice" (Ps. 141:2).

The next day Rosanna and I went to visit Annabelle to share our wonderful news. At this time of her illness, she was confined to her bed a large part of the time. What a thrill it was to tell her Paul had been touched by the Lord, that he had been completely healed, and that the Lord had given us a word for her. Tears of joy flowed down her cheeks as we rejoiced together, then she asked: "What has the Lord told you concerning me?" "Just these words," I remarked, "Annabelle is next!"

When I spoke these words, the most amazing thing happened: a powerful magnetism came into my hands—literally pulling them to her head. With astonishment I looked at Rosanna and said, "We are to pray for her!" I wondered, *How do I do this?* Then the Holy Spirit gently prompted me to pray a simple prayer as Reverend Brubaker had prayed.

As I placed my hands on her head in obedience to the Lord's direction, I immediately heard a loud horrifying voice saying, "If you do this, she will be worse than ever before." I instantly knew that this was the voice of satan. I praise God that my walk with the Lord enabled me to discern my Shepherd's voice.

> *...and the sheep hear his voice: and he calleth his own sheep by name, and leadeth them out. And when he putteth forth his own sheep, he goeth before them, and the sheep follow him: for they know his voice* (John 10:3-4).

I knew what I felt in my hands was the power of God; this was a strange mesmerizing moment of sacredness. There was no doubt that the sweet presence of Jesus virtually encompassed the three of us. Rosanna had also heard satan's voice.

I prayed a simple prayer of faith, asking for her healing through the name of Jesus, giving her time for confession of any known sin. She felt she had nothing standing between her and the Lord, so we simply thanked Him and closed with an "Amen."

She asked us to take her by the hand and help her to walk. Rosanna and I helped her out of bed; and as she put her weight on her feet, an excruciating pain struck her in the side. I almost yielded my faith to the voice I had heard moments before. But I recalled the Scripture in Second Timothy 1:7: "For God hath not given us the spirit of fear; but of power, and of love, and of a sound mind."

When we got to the sofa in the living room and sat down, the golden glow of God's presence filled the place as it had our own living room two days before. "This is God!" she whispered in awe. Just as Peter confessed "Thou art the Christ" in Matthew 16:16 and Jesus told Peter that flesh and blood had not revealed this truth to him (Mt. 16:17), even so flesh and blood had no part in the marvelous supernatural happening the three of us experienced.

On the way home, satan, who is the accuser of the brethren, troubled me. I felt as if some little demon was perched on my shoulder saying, "Don't you know that only the elders of your church pray for the sick? You are only a woman, how dare you pray for the sick, what audacity from a mere woman!"

When I went into the kitchen, I found Paul sitting at the table reading from the Bible. I leaned over him to see that he was reading from Mark 16. My eyes fell on the seventeenth verse, and I began to read:

And these signs shall follow them that believe; In My name shall they cast out devils; they shall speak with new tongues; they shall take up serpents; and if they drink any deadly thing, it shall not hurt them; they shall lay hands on the sick, and they shall recover (Mark 16:17-18).

A well of pure peace surged over my soul like a flowing river as I rejoiced in Christ my Savior. It stirred my soul to realize that my Lord had used me as a channel for His power.

When I awoke the next morning, I was tightly pressing my hands over my abdominal area. What an unusual way to awaken! I was strangely puzzled. As dawn brought in the new day, a new illumination from the Holy Spirit flooded my mind: "Claim your healing; it's for you too!" Fairly leaping out of bed, I stooped and knew immediately that my mass of adhesions was gone. I no longer felt any discomfort while doing the things I had previously been unable to do. When I had my next examination, the doctor could find no abnormality. What can I say but Hallelujah, what a Savior!

During these days we experienced a great thirst for the Word. It seemed as if every passage we read revealed some new truth we had never grasped before. We felt a compelling urgency to be about our Father's business. A fresh vision and burden for the lost engulfed our thoughts. We found it impossible to contain our exuberance and joy in Jesus Christ as our cup overflowed to everyone we met. We found a verse in Matthew that was like a command to us:

> *And as ye go, preach, saying, The kingdom of heaven is at hand. Heal the sick, cleanse the lepers, raise the dead, cast out devils: freely ye have received, freely give* (Matthew 10:7-8).

Was there anyone who had received more of God's mercy than we had? We owed so much to the Lord who had delivered us from our helpless circumstances!

Several days after our healings, Edith, a minister's widow who lived in my mother's apartment building heard about Annabelle's healing. She called to ask if we would come and pray for her emphysema. Edith had been hospitalized twice that winter. We went in faith and trusted in the promises we found in the Gospel of Mark. Again the Lord blessed as the power of Jesus touched her lungs. This was the beginning of our walk in the Spirit—believing the Lord to use us as an extension of His life. Our ultimate goal was to do His will and lift up His name that all men might know the Christ who had become real in our lives.

The Lord has anointed us to bring healing to many persons. One of the most remarkable was from a prayer request for Chris Shervanick. The teenager was hit while riding home from school on his bicycle. Chris's legs were broken and he was lying in a coma from his severe head injuries in the Intensive Care Unit of a local hospital. The doctors gave his parents no hope for any mental capacity should Chris awake from the coma.

Since these people were strangers to us, we sought the Lord's direction for our involvement. Two days later we felt we were to call the home. Mrs. Shervanick, eager for any hope, was ready to leave for the hospital, so she made plans to meet me in town. The Lord gave me a Scripture from Colossians 4:2, "Continue in prayer, and watch in the same with thanksgiving." These words were coupled with a "gift of faith" to believe for a miracle.

As I looked at the lad lying helpless in the bed connected to so much life-sustaining equipment, it was as if Jesus became alive inside of me. I took his limp hand and said, "Chris, Jesus knows what has happened and has sent me to pray for you." From the Lord, but through my lips came this command, "Awaken, my son, in the name of Jesus!" He squeezed our hands, the first sign of life. His mother was ecstatic! He clung tenaciously to us as I prayed, *Lord, what do I do now?* Then I heard the Holy Spirit say, "Pray for a natural sleep." As I prayed he gently released his grip and fell asleep. I was aware that the nurses knew something unusual had taken place as I quietly left the room. That afternoon the doctor realized a miracle had taken place and he was taken off the machines. When his parents came that evening, he was sitting up. He was in his right mind and had perfect coordination. Two days later x-rays revealed that the bones in his legs were also completely healed and he was sent home.

Before moving to Texas Chris and his mother stopped by to give their thanks once again for God's wonder-working power. Chris asked if I ever write a book to please include his story. With great joy I keep this promise.

Chapter 13

The Royal Robe

We were invited to attend a prayer meeting at Reverend Elmer Brubaker's home ten days after our visitation from the Lord. It was here that we witnessed a body of believers gather in spiritual unity with the evidence of Pentecostal power as described in the Book of Acts. We prayed fervently for the lost, for lukewarm Christians, for fresh anointings for ministers of the gospel, and for healing of the sick. It was truly exciting! Some were asking for empowerment to serve and referred to it as the "baptism of the Holy Spirit." We wondered, *Is this what we have experienced and why Christ is so real to us?*

By studying God's Word, we noticed that Jesus did not have a set pattern for the healings He performed while here on earth. One woman simply touched the hem of his garment and was healed. Another time Jesus took clay and spittle and anointed the eyes of someone who was blind. To some He spoke the Word, as in the case of the nobleman who only believed the words of Jesus and went home to find his son restored to health (see Jn. 4:46-54). It was humbling to realize He was choosing us to be vessels of His healing power.

Within the ten days since our visit, Annabelle had experienced a tremendous amount of healing, but satan was determined to have victory over her body. Before we left for the cottage prayer meeting, she called me on the telephone to pray for her, for it seemed that two forces were pulling at her. For five days she fasted, prayed, read her Bible, and had no appetite. This was no doubt providential to wean her body from the many medications she had been taking before this time. She requested that we have prayer for her victory when we arrived at the prayer meeting. After seeing a missionary, Stephen Fisher, sitting in proxy for his son, I asked that I might sit in prayer for my sister. During this prayer the Lord blessed me with a vision, which I believe is the most holy experience anyone could have on this side of eternity.

A vision with the magnitude of this revelation is almost impossible to describe. As we were praying, the missionary suggested that everyone also pray for us to be anointed for the ministry that we were about to be launched into. During the prayer I began to feel a warm penetrating light that hovered above me. It seemed to penetrate deep into the very marrow of my bones. It came with a soothing sensation and a purifying quality. As it drew closer to me, the light turned a soft rose color, and the nearer it came, the more crimson it became. Then it touched my shoulders and began to wrap about me like a robe of the purest red I have ever seen. Instantly, I felt the wetness of blood, freshly shed for me. A sensation of completeness engulfed me, along with a holiness, an inexpressible peace, and an overwhelming realization of the depth of His love for me.

I was overcome with my unworthiness and experienced an urgent desire to hide from His presence, so I covered my face with my hands and wept in His mighty presence. In these few moments of marvelous revelation of the sacrifice of His life for me, I became aware of so much I had never understood before. I now realized the price for my salvation through His atonement for my sins in an unexplainable measure. I also knew that His atonement provided healing for the body as well as for the soul of man. In the moments of that robing experience, I felt His divine protection, His authority and power, unspeakable joy, and His great glory. All that we have in Christ—His priceless righteousness for our eternal life—comes wrapped up in the glorious gift of our Savior's blood. Glory to the Lamb of God!

The vision lasted only a few moments. However, I arose from my chair a freshly-commissioned servant saved by grace, with a profound knowledge and faith kindled for time and eternity. Finally, I knew who I was in Christ Jesus my Lord. Ephesians 3:20 was no longer a mystery to me: "Now unto Him that is able to do exceeding abundantly above all that we ask or think, according to the power that worketh in us." Often I meditate upon this sacred and holy time with my Lord and wonder at His divine and vast love that He would choose me, such an ordinary woman, to reveal the powerful truth of His immense sacrifice to humanity. I can come to only one conclusion: there surely must be a work He desires for me to do. So as each new day dawns, I pray that He will use me to be a blessing. My service will never again be done out of a sense of duty, but from a commitment of love.

Three weeks later, because of a desire to show our appreciation to the Lord, my sister and I participated in a Love Feast and communion at her church. This was the church of our childhood days. What an emotional and exhilarating walk as she walked down the aisle without her four-footed cane. It seemed that all eyes were upon us. With our enhanced understanding of the blood sacrifice, this proved to be the most meaningful communion either of us had ever experienced. As we lifted the communion cup to our lips, we could scarcely swallow. How holy and sacred it had become! My sister enjoyed five healthy years after her miracle. Her doctor verified that this was not a remission.

Several weeks later the Lord taught me another lesson in a dream. I was standing knee-deep in quicksand and sinking. I immediately cried out, "Lord, save me." But I sank deeper, so I quickly laid flat on my back, but again I sank. Now I felt surely there was no hope for me as the soft muck and mire closed in upon me. Instantly, I was fully awake and very distressed. I questioned the Lord, "Is this what is going to happen to me?" Then I heard the name of a young man who was the son of a minister friend of ours. The last we had heard he was in New York City and not following the Lord. I slipped out of bed and onto my knees and began to plead with the Lord to save him. I prayed until I saw a cross appear, and on it I saw the bruised and battered body of my Lord. A calm came over me, and I knew the Lord had answered my pleas. This young man soon changed his ways, married a Christian girl, built a lovely home, and is respected in his church and community. With this dream came a new understanding of the word *lost* and an enormous sense of responsibility. I was learning that to whom much is given, much is also required. (see Lk. 12:48). Could just a short time of intercession change the course of one backslider from entering hell?

One day while balancing my checkbook, a heavy burden to go to prayer overwhelmed me. I had not the slightest idea who the need was for or what the trouble was. I began to pray; my spirit was in deep agony; and I wept with the travail of it, when suddenly I realized I was praying in a strange language. First Corinthians 14:2 tells us.

> *For he that speaketh in an unknown tongue speaketh not unto men, but unto God: for no man understandeth him; howbeit in the spirit he speaketh mysteries.*

Shortly after praying this way, my heavy burden lifted. I have never found who I was praying for, and that is of no significance. For I knew God required only my obedience.

One morning, not long after this incident, I received a mental picture of an ambulance with a flashing light at six o'clock in the morning. I began to pray, and later in the day I learned that my Aunt Mary had been admitted to the hospital for oxygen at that very time. Some may call these psychic powers; however, I strongly disagree. I was only obediently responding to the spirit of Jesus through the person of the Holy Spirit. John 14:21 explains it so well: "He that hath My commandments, and keepeth them, he it is that loveth Me: and he that loveth Me shall be loved of My Father, and I will love him, and will manifest Myself to him."

During our spring Love Feast service, one of the sisters of the church asked if we would pray for her brother who was in a local nursing home with cancer. At this time he was unable to speak due to brain damage caused by the cancer. After praying, we felt led to visit him. This lady and the man's wife took me to the hospital, and we prayed for his healing. Although he could not speak, we could tell he desperately wanted to tell us something. About two weeks later we learned that he had made no improvement and that his condition was deteriorating. I questioned the Lord where we had failed in bringing a blessing to this man.

His wife told me later that one day while visiting Jerry, his feet seemed cold and she gave him a paper and pencil and asked him to write if he wanted more cover. But instead of answering her question, he wrote—"PRAY." So we were asked to go again and pray for him, but in several more days he passed away. That night something very significant happened. It was near two o'clock in the morning. As the soft, gentle, June breezes refreshingly filtered over me through the open window, I was awakened by the strains of an angelic choir. It sounded like thousands of voices blending together in indescribable harmony. I was sure the rapture of the believers was taking place. I lay there waiting, and expecting to go through the ceiling any moment. But this was not as the Scripture had said, "In a moment, in the twinkling of an eye...we shall be changed" (1 Cor. 15:52). I could not understand, but I basked in the praises of this heavenly choir as it faded into the distance. Two hours later I was awakened with the same beautiful strains of music. This time it was more distant and did not last as long. In the morning I wondered why I had not wakened Paul to hear it also. That day I made visits to my next door neighbors to inquire if they had heard any unusual singing in the night, but no one had heard it. Paul felt the Lord was trying to tell me something. Later in the day I went to a friend's house and told her about the strange but beautiful singing. She questioned me if I knew someone who had recently died. As she spoke, the Holy Spirit softly whispered the name "Jerry." Then I understood that God had indeed answered the desire of this man's heart and that he was at home with the heavenly Father.

After sharing this with his wife, she revealed to me that he had carried a concern about the Lord's forgiveness in regard to an incident that had occurred early in his life. Then I understood that the ultimate blessing he was seeking was not for healing of the body but the desire for inner peace of God's forgiveness and for assurance of his eternal home.

This was a great and important lesson for us to learn in the ministry of healing as we desired to explicitly follow the Lord's leading into this gifting. Even the apostle Paul had sought the Lord three times for the removal of the thorn in the flesh; but because of the great revelations he had been given in spiritual matters, this was not granted, lest he "be exalted above measure" (2 Cor. 12:7). We must pray in faith but let God decide what is best for each person's life. The ultimate reason for a touch of healing from the Lord is not for us to just feel good or be released from our pain; rather, it is to give us healthy bodies to serve Him and have a testimony so we might glorify His name.

I have heard some say that testimonies should not be given, that it makes others feel inferior and exalts self. In the Gospel of Mark, when Jesus delivered the Gadarene from a legion of evil spirits, He told the man to go home and tell others what had happened.

Howbeit Jesus suffered him not, but saith unto him, Go home to thy friends, and tell them how great things the Lord hath done for thee, and hath had compassion on thee. And he departed, and began to publish in Decapolis how great things Jesus had done for him: and all men did marvel (Mark 5:19-20).

Many religious leaders will not welcome the verbal expressions of miraculous manifestations among their members; therefore, we have many cold, formal, and lifeless assemblies that do not meet the spiritual needs of the souls of our generation. Many we know and have learned to love have been made to feel unwelcome in their churches because they have witnessed miracle-working power in their lives. I am glad that I am not the judge of these who quench the Spirit of the living God, but I am sure He will not hold them guiltless in the day of judgment.

However, it is refreshing to know there is a growing number of churches willing to open their hearts and minds to what God has promised the church in these last days. Great revivals are sweeping across many foreign lands. With the increase of satan's last-day tactics, it is imperative that we know that the Bible has promised us God's power through the outpouring of His Holy Spirit.

Chapter 14

The Anvil of God's Word

In the summer of 1972, I awoke from a dream, speaking these words, "Do not drop the anvil; God wants you behind it." These words came with a prophetic anointing, and then I repeated them with questioning and consternation. Paul was awakened as I spoke out loud, and I asked him, "What is an anvil?" He explained it was a heavy tool often used by blacksmiths as they pounded and formed pieces of metal into usable shapes. The metal is heated over hot coals until it becomes soft and ready for shaping. Then it is made into instruments. In my dream I was standing in a huge octagon-shaped sanctuary in front of a large congregation of people. I had my Bible open in my hands; and as I stood watching, many of the people arose to their feet and walked out through the large number of doors around the eight sides of the church. The Holy Spirit caused me to understand the doors were avenues of service, and He spoke to me again, "Do not drop the anvil; God wants you behind it."

I could not understand the full impact of this call of God on my life until several days later as I was preparing a chalk talk for an upcoming church service. While going through my files of material, I came across a poem that made it possible for me to understand what the Lord had planned for my future.

The Anvil of God's Word

Last eve I passed beside a blacksmith's door,
And heard the anvil ring the vesper chime;

Then looking in, I saw upon the floor
Old hammers, worn with beating years of time.
"How many anvils have you had," said I,
"To wear and batter all these hammers so?"
"Just one," said he, and then, with twinkling eye,
"The anvil wears the hammers out, you know."
And so, thought I, the anvil of God's Word,
For ages skeptic blows have beat upon;
Yet, though the noise of falling blows are heard,
The anvil is unharmed—the hammers gone.

Author unknown

Many of God's chosen vessels have received direction and calls to service in a supernatural manner. Ezekiel saw the Shekinah Glory of God in a vision by the Chebar river. Joseph saw his brothers as shocks of wheat bowing down to him in a dream. Joseph also interpreted Pharaoh's dream of the fat and lean cattle that symbolized the years of plenty and famine.

I often pray that the Lord will help me be faithful to fulfill this call of teaching His Word. That summer my husband and I had many requests to share what the Lord had done for us and how He was teaching us to "walk in the Spirit." As the Lord promised in the Book of Mark, the Holy Spirit often accompanied our ministry with signs. This was a rewarding and awesome time of our life.

In the fall we were invited to spend a weekend with some friends in Lancaster County and go with them to a special evangelistic service. During the Sunday school hour, I had an overwhelming sense of the cold formality of this congregation. When we stood to sing the hymn at the beginning of the worship service, the Lord gave me an open vision. (An open vision is an event in which one sees and feels with both natural and spiritual senses.) Gentle spring raindrops began to fall on my arms and face, and I marveled at this strange occurrence. No one else was aware of the phenomenon, and I soon felt compelled to look around as I realized the rain was spreading throughout the sanctuary. We were singing the hymn "Spirit of the Living God, fall afresh on me." How truly it was falling, and yet no one was realizing the reality of it as I was. I thought, *We must be going to receive a very refreshing message from the Lord this morning.* Reverend Russel Bixler preached a tremendous sermon on the power for the Christian in using the name of Jesus.

At the close of the morning message, the Holy Spirit began to tell me something concerning these people that He wanted them to know. I knew it was somewhere in the Scriptures, and I said, "Lord, I will tell them if You can help me find it quickly." I found it in the Book of Malachi. Paul told me to go to the front and talk with the pastor. When the last song was finished, the minister said, "God has a word of prophecy for us this morning through our sister." Prophecy! Is that what was happening to me!? I was so overwhelmed, I began to weep as I went forward.

I first shared my vision of the refreshing shower of spring rain that had not only fallen on me but throughout their sanctuary at the beginning of the worship service. I was shocked at the strength of my voice as I opened my mouth to speak the message from the prophet Malachi:

> *Bring ye all the tithes into the storehouse, that there may be meat in Mine house, and prove Me now herewith, saith the Lord of hosts, if I will not open you the windows of heaven, and pour you out a blessing, that there shall not be room enough to receive it* (Malachi 3:10).

I knew that the prophetic ministry is to instruct, comfort, and edify the believers. This message met those requirements. As I took my place on the front pew, I felt as if every ounce of strength had left my legs. I had never witnessed persons moving in this gift of the Spirit; but then I remembered reading of Joel's prophecy in the Book of Acts:

> *And it shall come to pass in the last days, saith God, I will pour out of My Spirit upon all flesh: and your sons and your daughters shall prophesy, and your young men shall see visions, and your old men shall dream dreams: and on*

*My servants and on My handmaidens I will pour out in
those days of My Spirit; and they shall prophesy* (Acts
2:17-18).

Near Christmas we decided to go to the mall to shop. The carols lent a festive air to the occasion as we meandered from store to store. After selecting some Christmas cookie cutters, we went to the checkout where the woman attendant was wearing a heavy neckbrace.

The Lord spoke to me so plainly, "Pray for her." I knew I must be obedient, but there was a line of people waiting to pay for their purchases. I stepped out of line and told Paul that we were to pray for this lady. Perspiration seeped from my forehead and hands. We decided that we would come back for the cookie cutters later in the evening when she may not be so busy.

Later as we were in a book and card shop, my husband punched me in the ribs saying, "There she is!" I approached her as politely and tactfully as I knew how. There was not another person in sight. I explained that while in line at her cash register earlier in the evening the Lord had instructed me to pray for her neck. She smiled and told me that at that time my lapel button had brought conviction to her heart. I normally did not wear such buttons, but it had been left on my coat from a former occasion. It read, "Be prepared Jesus is coming."

She said, "The message of your button spoke to my heart, and I am not prepared to meet the Lord." So there by the card rack I led her to accept Christ as her Savior and prayed for her neck. She started rejoicing as a tingling sensation went through her neck and body as we prayed. After a few brief remarks concerning finding a church to attend and encouraging her to read the Bible, she glanced at her watch. "Oh, it's time for me to be back at work; my break is over." Not only had the Holy Spirit prepared her heart with conviction, but He also arranged a time and place for us to be together in quietness so that her life could be changed. This incident reminds me of how the Spirit bade Philip go into the desert at

Gaza and join himself to a specific chariot so that the Ethiopian official would have someone to explain the way of salvation to him
(see Acts 8:26-39).

I find it exciting how Jesus can order our lives for His glory.
One plants, another waters, but it is God who gives the increase.

> *So then neither is he that planteth any thing, neither he that
> watereth; but God that giveth the increase. Now he that
> planteth and he that watereth are one: and every man shall
> receive his own reward according to his own labour. For
> we are labourers together with God: ye are God's hus-
> bandry, ye are God's building* (1 Corinthians 3:7-9).

Every person is a precious jewel in the eyes of our Creator. I
would like to tell you how real He made this truth to me in a
dream. In the dream I was standing outside of the building that we
use annually for camp meeting when I saw a terrible storm approaching. I was certain that unless the Lord protected me, I would
be destroyed by the monstrous, black, tornado-like cloud that was
sweeping toward me. It was then that I noticed that all around me
were many precious jewels. Many of them were set in watches,
broken, and in need of repair. Some of the watches had no faces,
others no hands, and some were mere empty cases with no working parts. By now I was feeling the mighty force of the winds as
they approached. Surely I would be caught up with the terrible
force! I thought, *I must do something with these precious jewels*,
so I hurriedly gathered my skirt in apron-like fashion and began to
scoop up the broken gems. I could feel the suction of the great
storm as it swept close to me. Then it changed its path and roared
menacingly on—just missing me and my apron full of precious
jewels.

The Lord showed me that the jewels were souls of the broken,
discouraged, cast-off lot of humanity that He wanted me to help
gather into His Kingdom. Later on in actual life, Paul and I ministered to several persons on that very spot who were indeed broken
and discouraged, and later they became fruitful persons in the
work of both church and missions.

When women clean house, we often go through our knick-knack drawers and jewelry boxes and discard all the unusable, tarnished, and broken items. Not so with Jesus. He sees the need to repair and transform even the worst of us. To the natural eye a diamond, when first placed in the hands of the cutter, appears no different than a common pebble. But as one diamond polisher in Amsterdam said, "A month of time can be spent holding a stone to the grinding wheel to bring out its brilliance, depending on the person of royalty that it is being refined for."

We are jewels of Jesus Christ. A royal priesthood should therefore expect the refining fires of purification. For many of us it takes a long polishing period for us to reflect His glory.

Three characteristics of the faithful remnant are mentioned in the Book of Malachi:

> *Then they that feared the Lord spake often one to another: and the Lord hearkened, and heard it, and a book of remembrance was written before Him for them that feared the Lord, and that thought upon His name. And they shall be mine, saith the Lord of hosts, in that day when I make up My jewels; and I will spare them, as a man spareth his own son that serveth him* (Malachi 3:16-17).

There is a song I have always loved in our hymnal, written by George F. Root and W.O. Cushing that states this very well.

When He Cometh

When He cometh, when He cometh
To make up His jewels
All His jewels, precious jewels
His loved and His own.

He will gather, He will gather
The gems for His kingdom
All the pure ones, all the bright ones
His loved and His own.

Little children, little children
Who love their redeemer

Are the jewels, precious jewels,
His loved and His own.

Chorus—
Like the stars of the morning
His bright crown adorning
They shall shine in their beauty
Bright gems for His crown.

During this period of learning about many things concerning the outpouring of the Holy Spirit for the last days, we met others in our community and neighboring churches who were also being blessed with the anointing of the Holy Spirit. We felt a need to bring these persons together for sharing, prayer, and the study of the Word. There were many lay persons, as well as ministers, who had received the blessing or were seeking to come into the experience. Consequently, we opened our home to this fellowship of believers. We had from six to 60 persons meeting every other week for a period of three years.

We supported each other because many persons could not comprehend these new happenings, and we often met with difficult pressures from our respective church bodies. This fellowship proved to be a great help to each of us, and in time many of these persons chose to start home groups of their own to nurture other persons who were receiving the baptism of the Holy Spirit within their own circle of family and friends.

One evening a family had a flat tire on their car near the front of our house. Paul had the tools they needed and lent them a hand. We discovered they were new to our area and were looking for a church where the gifts of the Spirit were in operation. We suggested a local Assembly of God and also invited them to our home prayer group.

Two weeks later they arrived just as the last persons were leaving the house. The man had to close his shop that night, and so they were unable to come earlier. We invited them in for a visit. They had two children, a little three-year-old boy and a baby who looked the very picture of death. He was six months old and weighed only six ounces more than he had at birth. He was to be fed a special formula, but the mother said their finances were depleted and they had no money to buy more.

It was now after midnight, and the baby was crying with what sounded to me to be a cry of hunger. I suggested that if she had no milk at home and could not purchase any that I would fill the bottle with regular milk. Given her approval to fill the bottle, I went to the kitchen, washed, filled, and warmed the bottle. While doing this I prayed, "Lord, help us to know what to do for this emaciated little one." Before me came a long, white banner with the word *witchcraft*.

As I returned to the living room with the bottle and came near to the baby, he began to convulse. The mother in panic said she had never seen him like this before. It was then that I felt the power of God and the forces of satan overwhelm me at the same time. I told her the child was not able to grow because of witchcraft. The father was in the process of sharing with Paul that they had been living with a grandmother and a brother who were practicing witchcraft, and that was why they had moved out of the Harrisburg area.

We laid hands on the little one and commanded satan to loose the baby. We asked for the healing power of Jesus to heal his little body. His convulsing stopped immediately, and he drank the bottle of milk. The other little boy curled up on the carpet and went to sleep. We ministered to this couple until three o'clock in the morning. Within a few months, the baby's weight was up to normal.

When they left our area for a better job, they came to tell us good-bye. At Christmas we received a letter from North Carolina, stating that all was well and that they were happy to be serving the Lord in a church there. This was our first experience with deliverance.

In 1974 we received our first invitation to a Lay Witness Mission, which is a non-denominational ministry with the Institute of Church Renewal. At this time we did not know much about this ministry; however, my mother's church had a mission, and I attended the Saturday morning coffee hour, which met in small groups to discuss the importance and impact of prayer on a Christian's life. After hearing some of our testimony, the team person in charge of our coffee hour requested my permission to give Paul's name and my name to the person coordinating the weekend mission. She felt we could be an asset to the ministry of Lay Witness Missions. Paul and I knew we were already busy in the Lord's work and sought His will concerning this invitation.

Paul wanted to hear from the Lord so that we would not make a mistake. That night Paul saw in a dream a huge banquet table set with heavy china and crude place settings of silver. The meal had already been eaten, and he and a stranger were clearing the table. When Paul awoke he wondered about the unusual dream. Then in his spirit he knew that it was a spiritual banquet that he had been assisting with and that he was sharing the work with someone he had never met. The Hanover mission had 40 persons on the team, all of whom were strangers to us.

After this definite direction from the Lord, we accepted the invitation with great anticipation. This was the first of many missions over the years ministering to persons about the Lord and teaching others how to share their faith in Christ. We praise God for the opportunity to be a part of this important ministry to laymen. Our family of God increases yearly as we meet new friends in the larger Body of Christ and hear new testimonies of God's great power among His children.

Lay Witness weekends and Abundant Life weekends are a 42-hour witnessing experience. This includes the time spent in the church, the Saturday morning coffee session, and the ministry that occurs within the hosting families. The success of the weekend depends largely on the prayer foundation that is laid by the hosting church, the coordinator, and his team. It is amazing how the Lord arranges for team members to be placed in homes where there are needs which the visitor has already experienced in his or her own life, and thereby is able to minister to those needs.

While staying in our assigned home in Wilmington, Delaware, we learned this family's 20-year-old daughter, Susan, had been diagnosed with a rare muscle disease with no known cure. She had been an athletic young woman, involved in sports, but now she could not even walk without crutches. She was discouraged and felt her life was without hope. We waited for an opportune time to encourage her faith by sharing our healing and praying with her. After the Saturday night service, we had a time of devotions and sharing at her bedside, and then we prayed for her healing. She was happy to know God still touches people. However, because she did not know us, she was hesitant to reach out for a miracle. Although we saw no manifestation of healing, we were excited because we knew in our hearts that God had placed us in this home for her healing. It was difficult to leave Susan behind on Sunday morning, for months earlier she had been an integral part of planning this mission.

While we were at church, one of her friends stopped by for a visit. Because the girls had grown up together and had been friends throughout their school days, Kathy had heard of Susan's illness and came to encourage her. For three hours she shared her knowledge of Jesus and His healing power. Susan not only trusted this friend; she also knew that God was confirming our stories of the night before. She received her miracle, and not long after that joined her brother in Colorado where he was pastoring a church and needed her assistance with the work.

On another mission in Virginia, we were placed with the senior pastor and his family. His daughter Robin gave up her lovely canopied bed for our stay. The members of this church were hospitable and friendly. At the Saturday evening team meeting, the minister said the Lord wanted him to take several of the team to their sister church on Sunday morning where he also helped with the ministry. He said, "The Lord has shown me who I am to take, and I feel that you also know who you are. Please see me after the evening service." Paul and I both felt the finger of God point us out. After most everyone had left the church, we went to the minister and asked if we were the ones God had indicated. "Yes," he said. "It is you."

The next morning at four o'clock, I was awakened abruptly and sat up in bed. The Lord showed me in a vision the sanctuary at

Columbia Furnace. The lovely rose carpet, the white balcony, and the pews were just as I saw them the day before. But in the pews, instead of people there were small, lovely fruit trees. The fruit on the trees were of different varieties, quite sparse, and most of it was small and poorly formed. Then I heard the Lord speaking, "I am disappointed with the fruitbearing of My people, and I want you to tell them what is wrong. They are living too close to the world. Tell them to come into the sunlight of My love. There is also a drought among My people, for they do not drink of the refreshing water of My Spirit or receive the fertilizer of My written Word."

Next I heard His instruction, "Then stretch forth your hand to My people, for I want to bless them." I responded quickly, "Lord, I cannot do that, for I am not a man like Moses or a great man of old." His fatherly voice came back to me, "If you are obedient unto Me, I will bless thee also." I asked the Lord for a Scripture, and on the way to the kitchen of Sister Day to ask to be excused from breakfast, He gave me John 15:7-8:

If ye abide in Me, and My words abide in you, ye shall ask what ye will, and it shall be done until you. Herein is My Father glorified, that ye bear much fruit; so shall ye be My disciples.

When we arrived at the sister church, the minister announced that the congregation would not be using the prepared bulletin, for the Lord had shown him that some changes were to be made in the service. He also explained that he had prepared a message, but the Holy Spirit had directed him to give it another time. He announced he was going to read two verses of Scripture the Lord had prompted him to give to the congregation. With intense emotion, I listened as he began to read the two verses from John 15 God had spoken to me that morning. I wept out loud at the marvelous works of God.

When it came time for me to witness, I shared my vision, explaining that the Lord must have a special love for the people at this church. When it came time for me to stretch my hand to the people, the Lord told me to lead them in prayer. In my heart I knew that no one there was seeing me stretch out my hand. Through this I learned that the Holy Spirit will never let us make a fool of ourselves when He asks for obedience. Blessed be the name of the Lord!

We were then taken to the larger church where we had ministered, the one I had seen in the vision. Again I shared the vision and the message, knowing that the Lord was doing work in the hearts of these people. We were asked to minister in this church many years later, and we found that the people remembered the morning God had told them about their fruitbearing.

We rejoice in the marvelous works we have been able to share through the ministry of the Lay Witness Missions and the Abundant Life weekends.

Chapter 15

Drinking the Cup of Suffering

The enemy strongly opposes the saints of God; however, God has given us many words for our encouragement.

Who shall separate us from the love of Christ? shall tribulation, or distress, or persecution, or famine, or nakedness, or peril, or sword? As it is written, For Thy sake we are killed all the day long; we are accounted as sheep for the slaughter. Nay, in all these things we are more than conquerors through Him that loved us. For I am persuaded, that neither death, nor life, nor angels, nor principalities, nor powers, nor things present, nor things to come, nor height, nor depth, nor any other creature, shall be able to separate us from the love of God, which is in Christ Jesus our Lord (Romans 8:35-39).

In the winter of 1975, we were invited to minister to a home prayer group about 70 miles across the Tuscarora mountains. We were to speak Saturday night and for the Sunday worship service. We were warned there would be some resistance to our testimony at the church service, for a certain brother in the congregation did not believe that the healing and miracles that some experienced were from the Lord. He felt such things were from the devil, and therefore he was distributing literature among the brethren to substantiate his views.

We ministered to that congregation and returned home after an enjoyable Sunday afternoon with our host family. The next morning I was awakened about three o'clock with excruciating pains in my back. From the moment I was awakened with pain, a phrase began to constantly go through my mind: "As Jannes and Jambres withstood Moses." Over and over I repeated these words as they ground deeply into my mind. What did they mean, and why was I repeating these strange words?

We prayed asking the Lord for healing, but nothing happened. Consequently, we left for the hospital. I was admitted and immediately began to receive intravenous medication. My temperature soared as I shook the bed with chills until my teeth chattered. I felt too sick to pray, and I sensed that I was in a spiritual battle with the enemy of my soul. Tests determined that I had a kidney infection that had already entered my blood stream.

During the fifth night I was hospitalized, I heard a woman scream. She thought she was in a car and about to crash. I knew demonic powers were trying to destroy her. Anger rose up within me as I threw my feet over the bedside. *I must go and help her*, I thought. By this time I was reminded that I could not go anywhere attached to all my tubes. So I prayed that the Lord would send me a nurse who would take me to her bedside.

A few minutes later, the head nurse walked in. Seeing me sitting on the edge of the bed at that time of the night, she wondered what was wrong. I told her I wanted to go to the woman who was screaming, for I believed she was tormented by demon spirits. Suddenly realizing this was not possible or appropriate, I asked if she would pray with me. She said she realized that God was doing a wonderful work in deliverance through some persons and that she would indeed join me. As we prayed, the patient became quiet.

Once later in the night, I heard the woman cry out again, and I started to rebuke satan. Then I prayed that the Lord would soon finish the work, for I was very weak and tired. All grew quiet once more, strangely quiet. Then the Lord spoke to me, "Did you not say that you would drink of the cup that I drank of and be willing to be baptized with the baptism that I am baptized with?"

I said, "Yes Lord." Then I heard Him say, "I am pleased with you." It was then that I felt His touch and my fever broke. I fell into a very restful sleep, rejoicing in His presence, for I felt He was right there by my side. In the morning when I awoke, I realized that I was no longer repeating the phrase "as Jannes and Jambres withstood Moses." For five, long, weary days this phrase had gone through my mind like a broken record until I thought I would scream.

The next morning when Rosanna came home from her night shift at the hospital and was having her devotions, the Lord led her to a portion of Scripture in Matthew where Jesus healed Peter's mother-in-law. It read, "And He touched her hand, and the fever left her: and she arose, and ministered unto them" (Mt. 8:15). The Holy Spirit lifted Rosanna's burden and she knew she could break her fast, for the Lord had set me free.

After I was discharged from the hospital, my brother came to visit. I shared with Kenneth the strange words that rang through my mind. He opened the Bible to Second Timothy 3:1-15.

This know also, that in the last days perilous times shall come. For men shall be lovers of their own selves, covetous, boasters, proud, blasphemers, disobedient to parents, unthankful, unholy, without natural affection, trucebreakers, false accusers, incontinent, fierce, despisers of those that are good, traitors, heady, high minded, lovers of pleasures more than lovers of God; having a form of godliness, but denying the power thereof: from such turn away. For of this sort are they which creep into houses, and lead captive silly women laden with sins, led away with divers lusts, ever learning, and never able to come to the knowledge of the truth. Now as Jannes and Jambres withstood Moses, so do these also resist the truth: men of corrupt minds, reprobate concerning the faith. But they shall proceed no further: for their folly shall be manifest unto all men, as theirs also was. But thou hast fully known my doctrine, manner of life, purpose, faith, longsuffering, charity, patience, persecutions, afflictions, which came unto me at Antioch, at Iconium, at Lystra; what persecutions I endured: but out of them all the Lord delivered me. Yea, and all that will live godly in Christ Jesus shall suffer persecution. But evil men and seducers shall wax worse and worse, deceiving, and being deceived. But continue thou in the things which thou hast learned and hast been assured of, knowing of whom thou hast learned them; and that from a child thou hast known the holy scriptures, which are able to make thee wise unto salvation through faith which is in Christ Jesus (2 Timothy 3:1-15).

Moses stood against Jannes and Jambres, who were the leading necromancers of his day. Paul withstood the stonings, blasphemy, and persecutions of his time. We also know that Jesus' trials eclipsed all of these. How then could I not expect to drink from the cup of suffering also.

Several months later we were saddened to hear that the brother who thought he was doing God a service by resisting our testimony and the outpouring of the Holy Spirit in his church was crushed to death in the coal mine where he worked.

We serve not only a God of love and mercy but One who is sovereign and will not be mocked or have His work thwarted. Let us all have teachable spirits and be zealous in the Word, praying always for the Holy Spirit's illumination that we might rightly divide the word of truth. Through these things God taught me that I need not only divide the word of truth, but also use my God-given authority as part of my divine inheritance.

It is my sincere belief that to understand Jesus intimately, we must taste of suffering; and when the trial is over, we will understand more clearly His resurrection power. The apostle Paul prayed in Philippians 3:10, "That I may know Him, and the power of His resurrection, and the fellowship of His sufferings, being made conformable unto His death."

One night Rosanna was experiencing excruciating pain in her eyes. Since there was no previous problem or reason for her to be awakened from her sleep with pain, we discerned that the enemy was attacking. As we prayed together the pain was so severe she fainted. At first I was frightened, until I remembered I had authority over satan and his darts against us. Anger rose up inside of me and I commanded him to release her. It was then that I had a vision of Jesus' nail-scarred hands, held out for me to see. In each hand was a large, one-inch hole surrounded with blue and purplish bruises. I remembered the price He paid at Calvary and the authority I have to exercise against the enemy who would destroy the saints of God. As I stood my ground, the pain left Rosanna's eyes; and she went back to sleep. Nothing like that has ever manifested itself again.

Praise God for the teaching and the training I was receiving under the Holy Spirit's guidance.

Chapter 16

Dynamic Power

Since God is an all-powerful God and great in creativity, He often manifests that power in various ways. As a song writer wrote, "He is big enough to hold the mighty universe and yet is small enough to live within our heart."

As we contemplate the thunderings on Mount Sinai when God gave the Ten Commandments to the still small voice we hear at times when we wait for direction through the Holy Spirit, we can scarcely comprehend this marvelous power.

The great revivals of John Wesley, Charles Finney, and others in centuries past were accompanied by the miraculous power of God. During these supernatural movements, persons fell to the ground under the manifestation of God's power. Although it is not a Bible term, we sometimes hear this referred to as being "slain in the Spirit."

In the Gospels we read of Judas' betrayal of Jesus to the band of men and officers at the brook of Cedron. They came with lanterns, torches, and weapons to take Him. In this encounter, God's power caused them to move backward and fall to the ground. When Saul met Jesus on the road to Damascus, he fell to the ground as a great light shone upon him, transforming his life.

God's power has not been withdrawn. In this century we have heard of the phenomenal miracles in Kathryn Kuhlman's meetings, the meetings of the German evangelist Reinhart Bonnke in

Africa, and Gerald Derstine's missions to Israel. Derstine's revivals began in a small Bible school in Minnesota at the end of 1954. Pastor Derstine and his assistant met daily for prayer from 5:30—6:30 A.M. for a year, fasting on Wednesdays and Fridays so that God would send revival. There were phenomenal happenings as this revival occurred; many fell under the power of God and prophesied. These are recorded in *God's Visitation to the Mennonites*, *Following the Fire*, and *Fire over Israel* by Derstine. Paul and I have known the Derstines for more than two decades, and this revival has impacted our lives as well as many others we know. Truly the "Book of Acts" is being continued in our day!

Just as Jesus promised the disciples that signs and wonders would follow their ministry (see Mk. 16:15-18), we were learning that the same was true for us as we relied more and more on His wonder-working power.

One of those very special times occurred when we shared our testimony at the Gettysburg Full Gospel Business Men's Fellowship. As usual at the end of our testimony, we gave an invitation for salvation, healing, the baptism of the Holy Spirit, or any other prayer needs among the assembly. Approximately 30 persons came forward for prayer. There had been a wonderful time of worship in singing that evening, and we felt great unity among the people so that we were expecting the Lord to meet with us in a special move of the Spirit.

Paul knelt with a minister who needed prayer for the healing of his ankle. Paul had placed his hands on the man's ankle, and while praying the man fell backward to the floor. This happened to almost every person in the prayer line. It was a most humbling and awesome experience to be a part of such a powerful visitation to that group of people.

We searched the Scriptures to support this manifestation. If it was to accompany our ministry, we needed to understand the scriptural reasons for its occurrence.

> *It came even to pass, as the trumpeters and singers were as one, to make one sound to be heard in praising and thanking the Lord; and when they lifted up their voice with the*

trumpets and cymbals and instruments of musick, and praised the Lord, saying, For He is good; for His mercy endureth forever: that then the house was filled with a cloud, even the house of the Lord; so that the priests could not stand to minister by reason of the cloud: for the glory of the Lord had filled the house of God (2 Chronicles 5:13-14).

Notice that before the glory of the Lord filled the temple, the unity of praisers was as one. I am fully persuaded that the prerequisite for the glory of God to come down as we had experienced that night is unity among those assembled in praising and worshiping Almighty God.

One Sunday afternoon two couples came to our home for prayer. The older man had received a healing when we had shared at the Chambersburg Brethren in Christ Church several weeks earlier. Their son-in-law, Dick, had a serious heart condition. He had recently had open-heart surgery, and during the operation he suffered from massive bleeding. His wife was told that because of the condition of the heart, nothing more could be done to lengthen his life. So they came to seek help from the Lord. As we stood in a circle in our living room and joined hands in prayer, Paul's first words were an invitation to the Holy Spirit to be in our midst. Instantly, the mother-in-law fell backward on the sofa. Her husband became almost hysterical because he thought she was suffering a heart attack. We tried to tell him that she was okay and that the Lord was blessing her. We had not been told that she also needed healing for a condition for which she had been receiving therapy for several weeks at the local hospital.

After several minutes she began to praise the Lord and said that she had seen a little white cloud when we started to pray. It had come down to her, and now she knew that the Lord had touched her body with His healing power. Today the Great Physician was also the Master Therapist!

This manifestation of Jesus' presence augmented our faith and that of our visitors as we prayed for Sonja's long-standing back problem. There was a manifestation of God's power. Now finally it was Dick's turn for prayer! We saw no visible change, and he felt nothing happening; but when he returned to the city hospital, his surgeon wanted to know what had happened to make so great a change. Dick was soon out chopping wood for his fireplace and enjoying life again. The Lord gave him five more years before calling him home.

As I recall others who fell under God's great and dynamic power, I remember a minister's wife who lived in our neighborhood. During a prayer for inner peace, she shared that she saw a blackboard. On it were listed things that brought heartache, anxiety, and condemnation to her from her past life. As she looked at this board, she saw a hand move across the slate, wiping away each thing listed until the board was clear. I recall her countenance as she arose from the floor that day. Overwhelmed with peace, she wept with joy.

I believe our unbelief may be why we see so little of God's mighty power. When Jesus walked here on the earth, Scripture tells us He could not do many mighty things in His own country (Nazareth) because of their unbelief (see Mk. 6:4-6). Prophecy declares that in the last days many would have a form of godliness but deny the power thereof (see 2 Tim. 3:5).

In the writing of this book, it is my desire to bring the same message as found in Psalm 145:10-12: "All Thy works shall praise Thee, O Lord; and Thy saints shall bless Thee. They shall speak of the glory of Thy kingdom, and talk of Thy power; to make known to the sons of men His mighty acts, and the glorious majesty of His kingdom."

Chapter 17

Winds of the Spirit

Paul and I had many new and enlightening encounters with the Holy Spirit. There were phone calls for prayer and visitors who stopped by to share their experiences. It was exciting to be alive during this outpouring of the Spirit for revival! We felt fulfilled as we served others. We were finally witnessing all that we had longed for those many years.

There were few mundane or mediocre days. When they did come, we sometimes praised the Lord for the time to catch up on much needed rest and used the time for refreshing ourselves.

In the fall of 1972, Rosanna enrolled in a nursing program in Lancaster. There was housing in the dormitory for her first year of studies, but second-year students were responsible for finding their own housing. The local girls found housing within a short time, but we were concerned that Rosanna had not yet found an apartment.

One evening she phoned to say that she was going to check out a "for rent" ad in the city paper, five blocks from the hospital. Because I thought she was mature enough to make a good decision without us, I rested my mind. However, the next morning, I had a compelling feeling that I was to drive the 100 miles to help her with her decision about this apartment. To my utter dismay, when I arrived the dorm mother informed me that classes had been dismissed early and that she had left with a friend to see the apartment.

I was now in a quandary. I drove around and around a five-block area for a long time without finding her. Finally, in desperation, I began to look for a parking place where I could stop and pray. Since it was now evening and everyone had returned from work, I could find only one place to park. I sat there and prayed for quite some time; when I opened my eyes, I saw a lady sitting on a porch. I decided to give her a description of Rosanna and ask if she may have seen her go by.

The woman was friendly, and even though she had not seen Rosanna, she offered me a chair. I shared my predicament. "Is she a Christian?" she asked. "I have an empty third floor apartment and have been praying for a Christian woman."

She urged me to take the key and look through the apartment. It had large clean rooms nicely furnished with lovely antiques. Her rental fee was higher than what we felt we could afford. I thanked her for her kindness to me and stepped through her front door just in time to see Rosanna at the end of her front walk. It was an amazing shock for both of us. "Mamma, what are you doing over here, and at this house?" What a miraculous leading of our footsteps!

Rosanna was pleased with the apartment. We then asked the woman if she would consider allowing another student nurse share the apartment so that we could afford her price. We assured her that Rosanna's friend Celina was a quiet Christian also. For the next two years, they all proved to be a blessing to each other.

During the last year of Rosanna's schooling, she accompanied a group of doctors and nurses on a medical mission team to Honduras for three weeks. We were not aware that the Lord had spoken to her one night about going to a foreign land with the gospel. She felt this would be a way to sort out her feelings concerning the Lord's call to the mission field she had experienced at the age of 13.

When she returned home full of excitement, each new story she shared made us more aware of the possibility that she would indeed become a missionary. I wondered if I would be able to keep my promise to give her wholly to the Lord for His service. One particular story became stamped indelibly into my thoughts.

One afternoon Rosanna was taking a short break from helping the doctors with the long line of Honduran patients. Many of these patients had walked miles with small children and had become weary of waiting. As she surveyed their faces against the backdrop of the rugged mountains, a strange overwhelming love for these people rose up in her heart. She felt as if they were a part of her life. In those moments the vision and call to be a part of this harvest was forged deeply into her mind.

Also during these years, our church officials decided it was time to build another church at Upton. The old, hand-burned bricks were now porous, and the structure would no longer pass state inspection. We had grown in numbers and needed more worship and Sunday school space.

Because Paul was one of the church trustees, he was automatically part of the building committee. Since he had a mind for architecture, he drew up the plans after the men met and discussed what they wanted in a building.

Paul was also the treasurer, and he had a desire to see the church built without a large debt. The trustees decided to take loans from the congregation at a low interest rate and pay them back as the money came into the treasury. A bank loan was never needed, and the people of the congregation were blessed at being able to see what everyone's cooperation could achieve. The new Upton church was dedicated in 1976.

As the months rolled by, the winds of the Spirit kept blowing. New opportunities kept coming in rapid succession. We were asked to minister to a fellowship in Adams County. Many people there that day had also come into the renewal movement. Because it was a hot, humid day in August, the meeting was planned for the lawn. However, with the advent of thundershowers, everyone moved under the roof of the long porch which stretched the length of two sides of the rambling white house. We had a time of devotions, special music, and testimonies.

Paul spoke on the subject of "Broken Vessels." Many of us felt we were being refashioned as clay in the potter's hands. Our hostess asked me to speak to her friend from Philadelphia about her smoking habit. When I entered the living room, she had just lit a cigarette. Apparently she was convicted, for she soon disappeared. We have never felt that it is our responsibility to condemn people for their bad habits, for conviction is one of the works of the Holy Spirit, which results in the censoring of people's hearts as they see the Lord lifted up.

That convicting power also worked in the life of our host, for he approached Rosanna and me that day in the dining room and casually remarked, "I drink but it doesn't convict me." I realized the Holy Spirit was at work, and I said, "Brother, you must feel condemned or why would you be telling us that you drink?" He dropped his head and asked for us to pray for his habit.

As Rosanna and I prayed for his release from this addiction, I wanted to ask God to give him a thirst for milk and juices. Yet instead of saying what was in my mind, I began to speak words from the Lord; "Henceforth, my son, thou shalt thirst for the living water and the bread of life." Realizing the Lord had spoken, we all wept. Because the "gift of discernment" began to operate in Rosanna's spirit, she knew immediately what she needed to tell this man. We all realized the Lord was revealing something to her. Mr. Baker took her two hands in his big ones as he urged her, "Tell me what the Lord is showing you." She hesitated.

He insisted, "Come now, you must tell me. I really need to know!" Quietly she told him he must remove some objects from his home to be free from satanic oppression and to receive the blessings God had for him and his family. Her eyes quickly surveyed the room, and by the Holy Spirit's direction her finger pointed to three grotesque objects. I can only remember one of them, a statue of a hideous-looking monkey holding a human skull.

Without any hesitation, he gathered up each of the things indicated and carried them outside. When he came back, he knelt and began to praise the Lord right in the center of the room. Just then his wife Jean walked into the room. She was quite perplexed to witness this scene; but when we told her we believed the Lord was doing a cleansing work in her husband's life, she knelt and wept with him as he praised God with tears of repentance and joy.

After the evening service, this family began reflecting on the events of that day together. One of them remarked, "We should have taken the Negleys to that room upstairs that we cannot use." Apparently, when they bought the house, they discovered a foul odor in one of the bedrooms. It smelled very much like decaying flesh. Even the strongest cleaning detergents and deodorants could not destroy that smell. As a result, they always kept the door closed and were unable to use the room. They were informed later by a person in the community that someone had been killed in that house.

Although they had not told us of their problem, when they went upstairs to bed that night, they opened the door and to their amazement the foul odor was no longer there. Instead the strong aroma of old lavender sachet filled the air of the room. Many of you who read this account will have trouble understanding this, even as we do. We were thankful they had not thought to take us up to the room, for this way we were not given credit for this unusual happening. The blessing of this miracle can only be attributed to our mighty God who cares for His children when they clean up their lives. Within a year of this experience, this couple moved to an Indian reservation in New Mexico to serve as missionaries. Both of them were professionals in the medical field, but they gave up their high-paying jobs to follow in the new life to which God had called them.

This unusual happening served as a stepping stone for our ministry to a pastor of a Baptist church in Illinois. For our vacation that year, we decided to visit my father's cousin Lucille and her husband Harvey. Harvey worked closely with Pastor Jim, serving as a deacon in the work of the church in that small town, which was surrounded by flat, fertile acres of rich farm ground. Our cousins lived on one of these productive farms several miles outside of town. However, Harvey had found a way to put Christ and others first in his life. He and Lucille maintained their lovely farm

even with their business for the Lord, and their farm was even chosen as "Best-Kept Farm" of the year for a farmer's magazine. Beyond being relatives, their interests are very similar to ours, our
love for Christ and interests in farming bonding us together.

We had visited them five years earlier and shared our testimony with their congregation. Another minister was now serving
their church, and he and Harvey were quite a preacher-deacon
team. While we were visiting, Lucille and Harvey were anxious
for us to meet Pastor Jim and to share with him some of what the
Lord was doing in our lives. By our fifth and final day there, this
meeting had still not taken place. At the breakfast table Harvey
said, "I am going to phone them one more time." This time they
were home, and the minister agreed to come to the farm to meet us.
It was Harvey's intent for us to share of our blessings, but the Lord
had a different purpose in mind for our meeting.

We were all introduced then went to the living room and sat
down. Harvey commented that sometime when the pastor was not
too busy, he wished to hear what was happening in their parsonage. Pastor Jim said, "Well, I can tell you now. When we moved
here four years ago, we found strange things happening in our
home, like doors opening and closing of themselves. At times our
bed shakes violently, especially when I am away on church business. Often strange noises and sounds come from the basement
or under the porch. Once it sounded like two men were wrestling on the front porch; but when we investigated, we never saw
anything."

One night while his wife was alone lying quietly in bed, she
sensed the presence of someone in the room. As she looked up, she
saw a small boy clad in jeans and a red flannel shirt. When he
walked to the door, it opened by itself. Sometimes before hearing
these noises, they could smell a terrible odor coming from the corner of one of the rooms. He said he could not describe it, for it was
unlike anything they had ever smelled.

Paul and I looked at each other, and we remembered the
Adams County home back in Pennsylvania. What would the Lord
have us do? I excused myself and went to a bedroom to pray. After

praying awhile, I sensed the Lord's instructions to anoint the parsonage. The message was clear and simple, but how do we anoint something that is tangible? I knew we needed direction from the Bible. I prayed that God would show us what we should do through His Word. I turned to the concordance in my Bible and found under "anoint" Isaiah 21:5. The Lord had instructed the princes to anoint their shields prior to the anticipated invasion of Sennacherib's army. This satisfied me, for surely the parsonage was a necessary material part of the life of this man of God.

After conversing with Paul, we told the minister we felt God wanted us to go and anoint his home. Harvey drove us to the parsonage, which was several miles from the farm. No one would have guessed there was a demonic force troubling these people in this neat, clean, tastefully-furnished home. After meeting Pastor Jim's wife, we stood and prayed quietly in the kitchen. Each of us felt a reverential fear of the Lord's presence and the need for His divine direction.

"Do you have any olive oil?" we questioned. She did not, so she asked if furniture polish would do since it contained some oil. Apparently the Lord was not pleased with this suggestion, for He gave me a "word of knowledge." In a vision I saw a white medicine cabinet with an open door. In the cabinet was a small, thin bottle with the words "Sweet Oil" written on the label.

I told her, "Oh, the Lord just showed me you have oil for the ears." The wife went to the bathroom and came back with the bottle of oil, which I understand is basically olive oil. I believe God gives clear directions for His children as we strive to follow in complete obedience to His will.

The men took the oil, and as we walked from room to room the Holy Spirit showed us specific areas to place the oil. Our eyes seemed to stop at certain doors and areas. Then the Pastor's wife would comment about what would happen at each spot. She said, "That is the door that opens and shuts by itself." We felt an overwhelming sense of the power of evil as we entered the room where the bed would shake and levitate.

I fell to my knees at the foot of the bed, and we began to intercede for God's mighty power to bring peace to the resting place of this precious couple. We prayed for the complete cleansing of the house. The couple had shared that they often prayed when these things happened, but that it only lasted for a while. We asked the Lord to complete the work, and if we had failed to understand or had missed any part of this cleansing, we desired for Him to perfect what needed to be done. As far as we know this house was completely cleansed of this activity and has remained so to this day.

We returned to our cousins' house in reverential awe that Tuesday, speaking only in whispers. It is difficult to explain how unworthy one feels after such an encounter with the mighty God who is in control of our lives and directs us when we call upon Him for help.

We left almost a half day later than we had planned; however, it was good to listen and act on God's perfect plan for the day. Harvey said, "I feel like we should build up a pile of stones as a memorial, as they did in Joshua's day, so that we may never forget what God has done."

Chapter 18

Tocoa, Honduras

Life has been good to us, but it is attributable to the mercy and grace of our heavenly Father. It is amazing how our lives are entwined with the happenings of our children. One by one they enhance and add variety to the years.

We are grateful for each of our children's decisions to follow Christ at ages six and nine. Their lives reflect that those decisions were genuine. Those childhood years under our parental care had flown by so quickly. Now our lives were being filled with visions beyond those rural farm days together, for our children were making decisions concerning their future.

It was a day of pride as we witnessed Rosanna and her student friends stand on the stage holding the traditional Florence Nightingale candle and then file by, one by one, to receive their nursing diplomas. She seemed to be born with a personality to love and serve and was effective in her career.

The Christian youth group from Rosanna's high school decided to have a welcome home party for Isaac Burkholder, who had just completed a mission assignment in Honduras. We were surprised to see how much this once shy boy of 18 had matured into a tall, dark, handsome young man.

Rosanna and Isaac had a lot to talk about concerning their experiences in Honduras. Soon after the party, the group planned an autumn hike to the mountains. By this time, Isaac and Rosanna realized there was a special attraction between them, one that was different from that of their high school years.

After a year of dating, they were married in December of 1976. They had a Christmas candle-light wedding at Brandt's Church of the Brethren. The setting was beautiful. The ends of the pews were decorated with candelabra, red velvet bows, and pine. Red poinsettias, candelabra, and pine branches graced the altar. Her long white gown was simplistic but exquisite with tightly fitted bodice and long, flowing angel sleeves trimmed with lace. She wore a matching head-veil over her long black hair swept upward in an elegant coiffure.

Since Isaac was from the Mennonite church and Rosanna felt the importance of having Isaac as the spiritual head of the home, they decided to change her church affiliation during the wedding ceremony. Our minister, Kenneth Frey, gave her letter of transfer to Isaac's Uncle Aldus. Then after this transaction, she sang a song composed from the Book of Ruth in the Bible. After Ruth's husband and father-in-law died in her land, she made the decision to follow her mother-in-law Naomi back to Israel. Her words to Naomi have been set to music: "Thy people shall be my people and thy God my God, whithersoever thou goest, I will go." These moments were charged with emotion for both families as Rosanna struggled with the last stanzas of this sacred hymn. Rosanna and Isaac followed the song with their wedding vows in the presence of a church full of guests.

Isaac and Rosanna both continued to work at their jobs for a year before answering the Lord's call to go into missions. Since they both had experience with missions in Honduras, they applied for an assignment in that country.

After their papers were processed, they were assigned to Tocoa, Honduras. This was the area where Isaac had spent his three years with the Agriculture Project. Only this time they were sent to be the youth leaders of the Mennonite church in the town of Tocoa.

My test of being a missionary mother had finally arrived. Their dedication and commissioning day was January 2, 1978, at the

Pleasant View Mennonite Church. The minister's text that day came from a portion of Scripture relating to Jesus' ministry of preaching and healing in Galilee, and it is still applicable for today.

We took the children to the airport in Washington, D.C. on January 4, 1978, for their flight to Costa Rica. Our emotions ranged from excitement to deep despair, coupled with sadness. We knew we were blessed to have children who were answering the call to missions, but it was a frightening challenge to face years of separation. It would take weeks for letters to travel back and forth, and the telegraph service in Tocoa was set up in a shed no better than a chicken house.

As we sat in the waiting area for the final 90 minutes before their departure, many thoughts raced through our minds. Would the three-year assignment seem longer to them than to us when they had no other missionary friends or family to stand by them for support? As we sat in silence, the minutes ticked painfully away. Finally, the time for departure arrived. We exchanged our good-byes through half smiles as we fought back tears for each other.

After they went down the boarding ramp, we sat to watch the plane take off. Eventually we saw the plane taxi out the runway. We pressed our faces to the cold glass windows and watched the last glimmer of the plane's lights disappear into the blackness of the winter night. Tears ran down my face, and I felt Paul's arm slip around my shoulders. "Don't cry, honey," he whispered in my ear. "They are not alone, for the Lord is with them."

Rosanna and Isaac spent their first three months in language school in San Jose, Costa Rica. Isaac had already studied Spanish there for his first missions trip to Honduras.

The Holy Spirit comforted us during these early days while we adjusted to having the children so far from home. We were beginning to experience the pangs of separation when our first, much-welcomed letter arrived.

As part of their language study, they were to live with a native family. This was intended to teach them to communicate in

Spanish out of necessity. The family consisted of two parents, three children, three dogs, a cat, and a parakeet, all living in one tiny house.

It was a thrill to hear of God's special care in so many circumstances. Several weeks after they arrived, Isaac ripped a pair of trousers. Rosanna had not thought to pack a sewing kit for such an emergency. She was not yet acquainted with the stores of the city nor where she could buy a needle. The next Sunday morning as they walked down the street to the morning worship service, her eyes caught the glimmer of something shiny in the sunlight. Sure enough, there on the sidewalk was a perfect needle. My faith has been kindled many times as I remember this instance of God's provision for such a small detail.

After they finished language school, Isaac and Rosanna boarded an old plane out of San Jose and flew south to Tegucigalpa and then north to the city of La Ceiba, Honduras. While in flight they were caught in a violent thunderstorm. Lightning flashed and winds mercilessly tossed the antiquated craft to and fro. Rain pelted the plane until it came into the cabin. They prayed for God to keep them safe, for it seemed as if satan was trying to make sure they never would reach their destination. This was only one of the many times the Lord protected them and showed His mighty power.

Before leaving the United States, they were informed that there would be sufficient household supplies left behind by former missionaries to set up housekeeping. When they arrived in Costa Rica, they were told that everything had been sold and that they would need cooking utensils, dishes, silverware, bed linens, towels, and all incidentals needed for a home. There was a meager supply of furniture stored in La Ceiba that they were to use.

They sent us a letter with instructions to secure several heavy barrels to pack things in for overseas shipping. We spent many hours shopping and going through their household belongings to find supplies. This was a big job to make sure I had not forgotten something important.

Upon their arrival in La Ceiba, they were told that their barrels had come in by ship but that they could not be picked up until some future date. This type of scenario was arranged by government officials to secure bribes to pad their own pockets. But our heavenly Father had plans.

The head customs agent's car broke down soon after the barrels arrived. In Honduras automobile parts are hard to come by; consequently, the customs official was forced to turn to the mission school's mechanics. Because the missionary knew about the delay in releasing the barrels to Isaac and Rosanna, he informed the man that he would fix the car for a favor in return—the release of Burkholder's barrels. The car was repaired, and the barrels brought to them by mid-afternoon. How grateful they were for this divine intervention.

The men of the mission who were working in La Ceiba helped Isaac to load the mission's old well-worn pickup that afternoon. They had a bottled-gas stove, a kerosene refrigerator, a table and chairs, two beds, a dresser, and sofa. Finally, there was enough space to pack the three precious barrels.

After a night of much needed rest and a morning prayer meeting with the other missionaries for their protection, they set out on their 70-mile trip across rough, unpaved roads. It would be necessary for them to ford more than 50 streams where bridges had not yet been built to reach the remote town of Tocoa. Not far out from La Ceiba, the truck's radiator sprang a leak; at each stream they stopped to fill it up.

It had been two years since Isaac had traveled these roads. He soon found that the rough road had not been improved in that time, which resulted in several flat tires. After many weary hours of travel and numerous delays, they reached the mountainous terrain. It was now near nine o'clock at night, and their truck headlights went out. They knew they could go no farther until morning. However, when a passing vehicle came by, they decided to send a message with them to the Mennonite church in Tocoa, stating their difficulty. They ate supper of oranges and cheese from their grocery supply and tried to settle down for some sleep. It was near midnight when Rosanna was startled awake by car lights headed directly toward their vehicle. "Isaac, someone is going to run into us," she screamed. The men from the church had received their message, and they pulled to a stop directly in front of the truck.

When they went to work on the lights, they were surprised to find nothing wrong with them. The men said the bridge at the river was washed out. If they had gone farther, they would not have known to take the detour; and since the road was not barricaded, they surely would have driven into the river. What a wonderful God we have!

They arrived at the house in Tocoa at three o'clock in the morning. As Rosanna looked through the house, her eyes caught sight of a large snake skin lying on the fireplace mantel. Had the snake just shed it? This house had been empty for some time, but had been built and used by missionaries for over 25 years. It was a simple but adequate masonry house. The windows were without glass, but could be closed or opened by wooden shutters. After a good cleaning, it proved to be a quiet haven surrounded by young, fast-growing water coconut palms and banana trees. Isaac had planted the palms when he was there on his former assignment. Little did he dream then that one day he would bring his wife to this very spot to enjoy the shade from their branches as they swayed in the tropical winds.

There were two bedrooms, a dining room, an airy kitchen, a living room of ample size, and a lovely stone fireplace made from riverbed stones. A long porch was built on the north side. Blocks were built up half way, with iron bars above the wall for security reasons. This was a lovely cool place to tie up a hammock for a hot mid-afternoon siesta, for here in the lowlands the climate was hot and humid. Therefore, no one worked during the midday hours. Everything shut down, including stores. A clothesline was strung on the porch instead of outside so that no one would steal the clothes while drying. Robbery was a way of life here, even to the stealing of spouting from the house roof.

Once a thriving town made alive by American fruit companies that came to the area to grow bananas, Tocoa and the surrounding community had a population of 3,000. The fruit companies had built a railroad and electric system; but when crops were destroyed by a blight, they left the country. This brought everything to a halt, similar to the vacated mining towns of our country. Even the town hospital was without water or electricity; their yard fence was used to hang laundry.

A 15-year-old generator had been left behind by former missionaries, along with an old Maytag washing machine. Rosanna and Isaac were most grateful for these well-worn pieces of equipment and both were prayed over each day that they would continue to function. Sometimes they worked, and sometimes they stubbornly refused to work. When the rain barrel at the outside corner of the kitchen was empty, water was brought from the river. They were fortunate enough to have spouting on one side of the house, and the many tropical rains helped a great deal to supplement their water supply.

Isaac was the youth director at the Mennonite church, which had been established many years before. The church was built on a large lot behind their house. Near the church was a concrete block building, which was sometimes used for youth meetings on Saturday evenings. The youth group eventually grew to 60 members while they served in this capacity.

Just a few weeks after they were settled in, Rosanna came down with malaria. She was flown to the hospital at La Ceiba. This was a difficult time for her, for while struggling with the language and the culture she also had poor nursing care. God placed a burden on the heart of Diana (Dee) Brooks, a missionary from Michigan who lived in La Ceiba, to minister to her. Dee and her family are no longer on the foreign field, but they have remained steadfast friends, sending tokens of love through the years as encouragement.

With Rosanna's weakness from malaria, she found it necessary to hire a maid. A small woman in her forties, Pancha came once a week to scrub floors and do the heavier housecleaning tasks. Living along a dusty street with no window panes made for a lot of dust for each weekly cleaning.

Pancha was illiterate, but she came to know the Lord in a special way while working for our children; a close relationship was established between them. One day when Pancha did not show up as usual, they wondered what had happened. They felt something was wrong, for she had not sent word of illness or any reason for her absence. She was always dependable and punctual. Later in the day Isaac heard that her two sons had killed another man in a drunken brawl. There the law was "a tooth for a tooth, an eye for an eye." Under their law, this demanded a family member's life. For her safety, Pancha had slipped away in the night under cover of darkness.

One morning a small girl of about nine knocked at their door. She was shy and nervous as she handed Rosanna a note from Pancha. She had moved to another far-away town in Honduras. Rosanna asked the girl to return in half an hour for a package for Pancha. The child was frightened, fearing some trick was up to endanger her life.

After Rosanna assured her that she wanted to send Pancha a gift of love, she came back for the package. Rosanna had a bright pink sweater that the maid was fond of, so she quickly wrapped it with some money, a few toiletries, a Bible, and a letter. This was the last they heard from Pancha until a year later when Isaac returned to Tocoa on church business. While there, he heard someone call his name. To his delight it was Pancha. She told him of having terrible headaches after the murder, which she could not get over. But when she received the package with the Bible, she laid the Bible against her head, for she could not read it. She believed God would heal her headaches. She said they stopped immediately. She praised God that He loved her enough to do this tremendous healing in her body.

Rosanna and Isaac would love to return to Honduras once more and locate this dear Christian woman who meant so much to them during their two and a half years there.

My dental checkup that year also resulted in the blessing of many people in Honduras. As I was waiting for the dentist after the hygienist finished cleaning my teeth, the Lord gave me a "word of knowledge." It was a very simple directive, "Ask the doctor about going on a medical mission team."

Although I had known the dentist since the time he had first come to our town many years before, I was not one to expect him to use his time for conversation with his patients. However, I had learned that when the Lord spoke, I must be obedient; or I might cause people to lose the blessings of the Lord. In so doing I would also cheat myself of something He was planning. So when he entered the room, I told him that I needed to speak with him.

I clearly recall that moment. He sat down on his little round stool and pushed back. "Why sure, what is on your mind?" The Lord has just told me to ask you if you have ever thought of going on a medical missions team. His face lit up with excitement, as he said, "Are you kidding? For a year now I have been trying to go through the channels of my church without success."

I suggested I might have the address of the man who had coordinated the team Rosanna had worked with earlier in Honduras. When I returned home, I started a search through some of the children's files and found Lamar Stauffer's address and phone number.

Mr. Stauffer called the dentist's office that afternoon. The team was scheduled to leave in two months and still needed another dentist. God's plan was underway, and one doctor's desires were put into motion.

Dr. William Potts has been instrumental in involving other colleagues in this ministry. He has also been able to secure better equipment and supplies for the missionaries from pharmaceutical companies. One of these provisions includes a special dentist's field chair which is often carried on the back of a mule into remote areas. The dentist's wife, Peggy, accompanies him on his many trips to Honduras and Guatemala and works by his side. They have shared with us that this Christian outreach has enhanced their lives as they have blessed literally thousands of people.

I have found the gift of the "word of knowledge" to be a powerful tool in the work of the Kingdom. I pray that God will continue to give me the sensitivity to listen for His still small voice and the boldness I need to use the tools of the gifts of the Spirit. I want to be a channel for the Lord Jesus to flow through so that others will be blessed, for this, I find, is the fulfillment of my life.

This prayer was the desire of our children's hearts as they labored in Honduras. They grieved that so many persons did not have access to a Bible. Consequently, they decided that it would be necessary for them to start a bookstore in their home where Bibles and other Spanish literature could be purchased. They saved as much as possible from their meager salary and enlisted interest from family and friends back home to make this possible. Everything was sold at cost so that people could secure at least a part of the Scriptures.

One man in particular was so in earnest to have his own Bible that he walked for many miles to the store and insisted that he leave his watch for security until he could pay in full at a later time. One small booklet, "Biblical Prayer and Fasting," written by Robert Flory, was especially sought after and yielded many fruitful results. More than a decade later, requests are still being made for this booklet to be used in Honduras.

I am reminded of a vision that the Lord gave me to help me understand that what people may consider small and insignificant is not necessarily so in the eyes of the heavenly Father. In my vision I saw the trunk of a giant tree cut off a few feet above the ground. God gave me a picture of the tree's massive root network. There were large roots first, then they branched out into smaller and smaller ones until finally the inconceivable number of hair roots reached farther and farther from my view. The Holy Spirit helped me understand that what I saw was a picture of true ministry: one tiny, helping hand extended in love can grow under the multiplication and blessing of Almighty God. It may never be noticed by men, but it is not missed by the Lord.

Chapter 19

The Banana Express

We ventured our first flight to Honduras in February, 1979. The weather was cold, and a blanket of 15 inches of snow covered the ground. As we neared the Hagerstown, Maryland airport for our commuter flight to Washington, a thick fog moved in. After an hour delay, the Hagerstown terminal summoned a taxi to drive us the 100 miles to Washington, D.C. The rickety old taxi pulled into the airport's departure terminal with its five passengers and their mountains of luggage five minutes too late for us to catch our flight. This meant that we would spend a long, weary night at the Miami airport.

We passed a restless night, but dawn brought a refreshing excitement as we boarded the plane and headed south for Honduras. In a few hours we had a spectacular view of banana country as the plane circled over La Ceiba. We saw a vast carpet of green punctuated by huge geysers spouting water onto the banana fields. The acres and acres of pineapple fields were also a beautiful sight. So this was the country to which our children were called!

La Ceiba is a seaport town with a population of 75,000. This was the closest airport to the children, and it was the city to which they flew to transact all their major business and buy their supplies. However, Isaac had decided to rent a car in La Ceiba and drive on to San Pedro Sula to meet us so that we would get to see more of the country. As we flew on to San Pedro Sula, we were met with temperatures near 100 with high humidity. This was a shock after the cold winter and snow we had left in Pennsylvania.

As we hurried down the steps of the plane, we gazed longingly toward the huge glass windows of the terminal until we could see Rosanna and Isaac. They were brown from the tropical sunshine, healthy looking, and radiant with happiness. Tears of joy streamed down my cheeks as we waved to each other. We rejoiced that our luggage and all 200 pounds of their supplies had arrived safely.

After a refreshing sleep in San Pedro Sula, we headed back to La Ceiba over one of the country's three macadam roads. Now we had a closer look at the lush banana trees and pineapple fields. These large farms were operated by government-run cooperatives. Farther on we came to more hilly country where corn and beans were planted in small patches. The indigenous farmers used oxen and plows. What a contrast!

We had lunch in La Ceiba and made a trip to Capallades Grocery store where Rosanna and Isaac stocked up with their usual month's supply of food. We then boarded an old DC3 plane for our 60-mile flight to their home in Tocoa. As we flew, the body of the old plane seemed to vibrate from the agony of its age. We truly wondered if it would hold together, for we saw that it had already lost some of the bolts that held the wings in place.

As we circled over Tocoa for landing, we saw its few, narrow streets. They were lined by simple homes built with hand-poured cement blocks and roofed with tin. Other homes on the edge of this small town were made of bamboo mortared with mud with thatched roofs. Outside of town the Aguan river ribboned its way through the valley, bringing life and rich vegetation.

As we approached the airstrip, which was just a grassy country field, pigs and goats scurried away from the noise of the plane and its propellers. There was a jolt, several bumps, and then we came to a sudden halt. We were here at last!

Our skin looked pale in contrast to the Hondurans' dark brown skin and black hair. We wondered if the contrast made us appear sick and delicate to them. Their faces conveyed to us their hard and difficult way of life. They were smaller in stature than us, and they were thin from what we believed was insufficient nutrition. The men here had little opportunity for work other than tilling the soil, constructing their simple homes, and doing mechanical repair for the few vehicles in the neighborhood.

We found our children's home to be a haven of peace from the atmosphere of the community. The town taverns constantly vied for business with loud blaring rock music. There was no escape from the mix of worldly racket as it went on endlessly, day and night.

Not long after going to bed, we discovered that here the roosters crow every hour of the night. Long before dawn we heard the gasoline-powered corngrinder droning away as it ground the white lye-soaked corn for each family's daily tortillas. The cool dampness of the early morning silence was broken by the pit pat of children's and women's bare feet as they walked swiftly by the house on the way to and from the grinder. Pans of freshly ground cornmeal were balanced on their heads. Yet another sound that resounded through the town before daylight was the beep-beep of the horn on the government-operated truck. The truck picked up workers and transported them to the co-op farms on the outskirts of Tocoa. To us Tocoa was a place of strange sounds, for each morning we also heard the flump-flump of heavy wooden wheels of an ox-drawn cart as it came up from the river with its barrels of water. The driver sold the water for three lempiras, the equivalent of $1.50 a barrel. This was costly, for the men earned a mere seven to eight dollars per week.

Since Rosanna had been away for several days, we needed eggs for breakfast. Without adequate refrigeration, meats and perishable food were purchased in small quantities. We walked to a nearby house that was not only a dwelling but a butcher shop. From appearance, I would never have guessed. Eggs were gathered for sale by the proprietor from the ground. There were a few trees in the enclosed lot where the hens would, out of need for a nest, sit on the ground and deposit their egg for the day. The eggs were kept in a bushel-size woven basket since the store had no refrigeration. It was not unusual for Rosanna to find a rotten egg, or even worse, one with a partly developed chick. I had determined that I would not complain about this primitive way of life. However, it became very easy to suggest we have oatmeal and coffee for breakfast. Tuesday was the proprietor's butchering day. Rosanna would listen carefully that morning of the week until she heard a shot ring out across the way. After giving ample time for the man to butcher his hog, we would go to the house once again. Large pieces of pork would be lying on the table awaiting customers, still warm with animal heat. One could not buy pork chops, ribs, or a loin roast. The butcher simply cut as many pounds as the customer wanted. He would raise his sharp machete, and with one whack, off came each customer's portion. It was crude indeed, but we were thankful we could get the meat fresh before the flies had much time to crawl over it.

On another day we went to a different butcher for beef. We were appalled to see a skinny cow standing nearby waiting to be slaughtered. This butcher's shop was just a slab of concrete with only a roof to ward off the sun and rain. Nothing in Honduras is ever wasted; one day I saw a small boy carry home a cow leg with the hair still intact. Rosanna said his mother would skin and clean it to make a soup. Later that week we saw another man hauling part of a butchered cow on a wheelbarrow. The complete head was there, and he intended that someone would purchase it, too. Although it was a gruesome sight, his meat was sold fast, for every day does not afford them an opportunity to buy meat. The man used an old-time balance scale to determine how many pounds he had chopped off.

The waste in America should make us hang our heads in shame. The main foods of the Honduran diet are rice and beans, supplemented with tomatoes, cabbage, carrots, and corn tortillas. Children with protruding stomachs due to malnutrition could be seen in every part of the country. Our hearts ached with compassion as we watched these people and their difficult way of life. The children had only a few homemade toys, and many had no opportunity to go to school.

On Sunday we went to the Mennonite church. The women greeted me warmly by extending their hand to touch my elbow, which is their traditional way of greeting. The men shook hands as we do here in the United States. Their warm smiles and glittering eyes indicated that we were expected and welcome.

Joyful singing and clapping enlivened the church service, and the sermon was occasionally interrupted to chase a community dog or two from the sanctuary. The continual noise of rock and roll music from the tavern across the street was a constant reminder of satan's presence as the pastor lifted his voice to override the interference.

The Hondurans had few diversions in their lives, for there was nothing in the way of sports or the arts available. An old theater, the taverns, and the town brothels provided them with little to choose from. Unless they had interest in a church group for fellowship, there was little of value for building character and moral restraint. Fathers or uncles were noted for introducing their boys to the houses of prostitution in their teen years. On a Saturday night it was a usual sight to see drunken men lying along the street where they had fallen, and they would stay there until they sobered up. These people surely needed to hear the gospel.

As we walked the streets, we were made aware of the tremendous satanic forces that prevailed over this community. For many years the most renowned witch doctor of Honduras lived and practiced in this area. He had brought death and bondage to many persons with his occult practices.

Isaac's link to the outside world was a two-way radio, which he operated daily for weather communications and business. On their last trip to town before our coming, they had called home and requested we pray for a two-year-old daughter of Mr. Crispi. This man was a staunch Christian and an official in the church in Tocoa. Little Marianna had a mysterious illness and had been flown into the capital hospital at Teguciagalpa. The doctors there had given up any hope for her survival. She had lost a lot of weight, most of her long black hair had fallen out, and she was experiencing other complications as well. These unusual cases were often attributed to satanic powers. God heard the prayers of this dear family, and Marianna returned to her home. Soon after our arrival, the Crispi family invited us to their home to have a praise service of thanksgiving for the healing of their daughter. Isaac had learned to love this family during his first trip to Honduras; and when one of the little boys was born, they named him Isacito, meaning little Isaac.

Death comes often in this country. Many times during our three-week stay, we heard the ringing of church bells, signaling to the community another death. A rough wooden box was put together within 24 hours to serve as a casket, which was then carried by the kin to the burying grounds at the edge of the town. Someone with a cross or garland of flowers followed the casket while the rest of the family followed in procession.

In the heart of Honduras' banana land, one can take a fascinating trip through a valley that is a little world of its own. Isaac was eager for Paul and me to have this overview of the country by riding the Banana Express. The narrow-gauge railroad, built in 1906, takes passengers along with more bananas than one has ever dreamed of on a day's journey through tiny towns and forests, over mountain ridges and streams.

One day we flew into La Ceiba and stayed overnight so that we could be at the train station at the crack of dawn, for we wanted to make sure we had good seats on the Banana Express. We discovered we would not have needed to rush because the train was not on time, nor was it ever on time for the remainder of our trip. These delays gave us time to survey the Honduran people and their way of life.

The valley through which we traveled had only jungle trails; therefore, the railroad tracks are its highway, with all the villages hugging the right of way. The open coach windows gave us a view of the community activities as we moved slowly along. Innumerable delays occurred while bananas were loaded and vendors accommodated.

Most of the Aguan natives have never been out of the valley. Their thatched houses were built near streams for their water supply. When the train stopped, we could see men taking their midday siestas in hammocks swung from branches of trees.

At many of the stops, women or girls came out of trails carrying baskets of eggs. Cornhusks were wrapped around the eggs to prevent breakage in transportation. Other women carried basket-like trays with hot and cold foods for meals on the train. Women offered prepared *chuletas* (steaks), empanadas, tortillas and hard boiled eggs, cooked yucca root, and chicken or fish.

There was much activity on the train at each stopping point along the way. The train was a veritable bazaar as vendors boarded the train to sell underwear, head scarves, toys, balloons, pocket combs, household gadgets, and jewelry. It looked like a moving variety store.

This dramatic and scenic trip provided many spectacular views, for the train crossed deep canyons over high trestle bridges. Much prayer accompanied our viewing as we looked down on waterfalls or rounded a curve and looked back to see the end of the train crossing a flimsy bridge high above a deep ravine.

After ten hours on this excursion, we disembarked in a small village and walked to the river. Here we met others who were waiting for the next cayuca (dug-out canoe). We intended to cross to the opposite side and get a taxi to take us to Tocoa. The antiquated canoe was hollowed out of a giant tree with a small motor attached for power. The men helped Rosanna and me down the steep riverbank and into the already overcrowded conveyance. There were two dozen persons, a bicycle, treadle sewing machine, many boxes, and bags of provisions from the city. Rosanna and I were near the middle of the boat, which was now all but dipping in water. She cautioned me to keep down low on my knees and hold on tight. We made it safely across; however, the following week three persons lost their lives here in this crossing. Life in Honduras is cheap because accidents happen often and are taken for granted as a way of life.

Once across the river everyone made a mad scramble for the waiting taxis. Isaac tried to arrange for one of the drivers to give me a place in the cab of his Toyota pickup. Others had the same idea, so I was the last of three women plus the driver for the front seat. I drew in my breath so the driver could latch the door. On my feet I held a large *bolsa* (bag) of groceries plus a box on my lap. Twenty persons either rode or hung on the back of this lightweight truck as we bumped along a windy, rough dirt road.

It was a blessing to be in Tocoa with the children and share in the experiences, both good and bad, and learn more about the work there. During the second week, we were invited to share our testimony at the Wednesday evening service. It was our first time to share with the people here, and Isaac served as our interpreter. At the close of the service, Mr. Crispi asked for prayer for his eyes and encouraged others to come forward who desired prayer for healing.

Many came forward; among them was a woman asking prayer for her husband's salvation. He had been on a three-week binge at the local tavern. She had put a "fleece" before the Lord. If he came home sober after being drunk for so long, she would know this would be a supernatural sign for her to set up an evening of ministry with the Burkholders at her home. Amazingly enough, he did come home sober, so an appointment was made for a house meeting on Friday night.

Friday night after supper was finished, Isaac lit the Coleman lantern to light the way down the dusty, dark street toward the river. The rustling of the palm trees blowing in the night air along both sides of the street still sound in my memory. We passed several other bamboo and mud houses until we arrived at this woman's humble home. The living quarters were sparsely furnished with a small table, which held a kerosene lamp, plus several chairs and a bench.

As their special guests, we were given the chairs while Isaac shared the bench with the woman's husband as he read from the Bible. Others sat on the cleanly-swept floor. All nine of their children were present. Neighbors and friends gazed attentively through the open windows and door.

An expectancy filled the atmosphere that something was about to happen. These people were hungry to hear the gospel and understood that the mother was expecting God to do wonders for her addicted husband. Although Isaac had not yet been licensed to the ministry, the Lord was using him to touch lives. We sang several hymns and then Isaac preached a short evangelistic sermon. Paul and I followed this by sharing a portion of our testimony of God's touch of healing in our lives.

Sunday night we were amazed to see many persons at church whom we had not met previously. Among them was the former drunk, now in sound mind who came forward to accept Christ as his Savior. He was delivered from his alcoholism and remained faithful to his commitment to Christ according to our last contact. This was a night to remember as we saw many touched with the mighty power of God.

One lady in the prayer line laid my hand to her midriff to feel the constant trembling she had long endured. By a word of knowledge the Holy Spirit led me to know she had sought help from a witch doctor. I asked Isaac to inquire of her if this was correct.

"Yes," she said, "I did not know this was a bad thing to do in God's eyes." She raised her hands, and in great anguish wept in repentance. Never before had we witnessed such sincere confession. This shaking in her stomach had tormented her for years. We took authority over the powers of satan, and she received an instantaneous miracle as the shaking ceased.

We realized the childlike faith of these people was unhindered by traditions or theology. They believed that there was a good and bad spirit world, and they simply accepted by faith that God could heal their diseases.

Also at the altar for healing was a young man with a long-standing infection on his chest from a machete wound. Paul told Isaac to tell him that if he gave his heart to the Lord, he would receive healing. He unhesitatingly accepted Christ that night. Several days later he came to the house, bared his chest to the men, and showed them what God had done for him. He was healed even without scars! The next evening he showed up at the church to help load chairs to take along to a scheduled meeting in an outlying area. This kind of commitment revealed he truly experienced a transformation of heart.

Many more miracles happened that night at the little Mennonite church in Tocoa. A 16-year-old neighbor girl was gloriously delivered from epileptic seizures. A frail little girl about 12 years old with severely impaired breathing from asthma, or some similar disease, was healed. What a soul-thrilling experience to lay your hands on a small heaving chest and feel the touch of Jesus change her every breath until she breathed normally. Her little face glowed as she felt the power of Jesus touch and heal her lungs. We have learned the reality of Paul's words in his Epistle to the Ephesians:

> *Now unto Him that is able to do exceeding abundantly above all that we ask or think, **according to the power that worketh in us**, unto Him be glory in the church by Christ Jesus throughout all ages, world without end. Amen* (Ephesians 3:20-21).

During the last night of services in Tocoa, the church was overflowing. People stood around the walls, waiting and believing God for their miracle, for the word of God's outpouring of the Spirit had been spread throughout the area. That night many came forward when the invitation was given. Many mothers brought their babies to the altar. We believed some came for the child to receive a blessing, while others were unquestionably sick. This was an evening we will never forget, for the mothers pressed into us with outstretched arms holding out their little ones. With practically no help from physicians or even minor medications, in this area illnesses often resulted in death.

In this hour of faith testing, we felt so unworthy. "Dear Father," we prayed, "flow through us with Your power that the many needs of these people will be met." It is an awesome and humbling experience to sense the flow of God's power as He saves, touches, heals, and performs such mighty miracles before your eyes.

The three weeks in Honduras went all too fast as we worked with the children. Before we left for home, they wanted us to see the white beach at Trujillo. We drove three hours over rough, muddy roads in remote territory. While fording a stream in a thickly-wooded area, we were privileged to see a family of monkeys gleefully swinging from tree to tree.

We reached the port town of Trujillo with its abandoned forts. This was a small Spanish town with the usual Catholic church, bank, restaurant, and tavern. Isaac pulled the pickup truck down a narrow street to the white sands of the shoreline. The miles of beaches lined with palm trees swaying in the ocean breeze were truly breathtaking. The water was clear and sparkling blue. Best of all, there was not a person in sight for as far as we could see. This truly was a bit of heaven on earth.

As we returned to Tocoa, we enjoyed a magnificent sunset, outlined by the black silhouettes of palm trees along the way. No artist could ever have captured the exquisite colors of this sunset or the gorgeous beauty of those pristine beaches at Trujillo.

Parting at the airport was difficult, but we all rejoiced that the Lord had blessed our time together in such special ways. Our hearts were strangely knit to these people, and we knew we would want to return someday.

Chapter 20

San Marcos

Christmas of 1979 was a time of rejoicing for our family. Katrina arrived home safely from her semester of art studies in Europe. Rosanna and Isaac also returned to the States for a month of rest before their next assignment in San Marcos, Ocotepeque, in western Honduras. She had a real surprise for us, for she was expecting a baby. Shannon's three sons Marvin, Darrell, and Lee were already adding joy to our lives. We praised the Lord for love of family as we joined together to celebrate the birth of Jesus.

January brought the scattering of the family once again. Katrina was enrolled at Indiana University of Pennsylvania for further studies in art. Rosanna and Isaac went back to Tocoa to move their furniture to their next mission assignment, which was just across the border from El Salvador.

Because January through March is Honduras' rainy season, this complicated their moving plans. Some of their furniture was air-lifted to La Ceiba, but most of it was loaded onto a cattle truck. They joined the driver for this rough 13-hour ride. This was not a wise decision for Rosanna's condition, and after the long ride, she went into labor. The women from the church came and prayed for her, and the premature contractions stopped.

One month later they made the six-hour trip north to San Pedro Sula. Here God provided a couple to open their hearts and home to them until the baby would be born and they could return to San Marcos. Mr. Manning was an American married to a Honduran woman. His wife was a lovely Christian woman who belonged to the Mennonite church in the city. She was a big-hearted woman who was active in all phases of church work. Mr. Manning served as the United States representative for a truck company. He and his crew of men traveled frequently to the United States to bring back new vehicles. His wife, Bonita, with her loving and generous spirit, was the spiritual leader of this family and had a great influence on many lives.

The Manning family lived in a prestigious home with three maidservants; one cooked, another cleaned and did laundry, and the third served as a nanny for the children. There was also a gardener, a chauffeur, and a guard for night duty, who walked constantly around their high-fenced lawn. The grounds were landscaped with palms, citrus trees, roses, and other beautiful flowers. Mr. Manning loved to barbecue and often served steak and chicken platters. He was a generous host and was highly offended when Isaac offered to pay for their stay.

Rosanna and Isaac appreciated a month of their hospitality until Nathaniel (meaning gift of God) was born. When the baby was five weeks old, I decided to go down to help them settle in San Marcos. Paul planned to join me in a month.

This was quite a trip for me to make alone. I was to arrive at Miami at midnight and be there for seven hours. I prayed that the Lord would provide a person for company during the trip from Florida. After I boarded the plane and no one had been seated in my section, I began to wonder if God was not going to grant my request. However, the last person who boarded was a sophisticated, dark-complexioned man. He greeted me warmly as he took the seat next to me.

Soon after taking off, I took my Bible from my handbag and began to read. "Oh, you are a Christian too, and, I might add, an answer to my prayer," he confided.

"That is most interesting," I remarked. He told me that at the airport the night before, several men had stalked him. After managing to lose them in the crowd, he prayed that God would provide

Christian fellowship for the rest of his trip. We talked about the goodness of the Lord in our lives.

He was a Honduran who had worked as a banker in New York for 20 years. Because his wife was seriously ill, he was returning home to buy a house where she could spend the rest of her days. I shared my husband's testimony of healing and showed him Scripture passages that supported the promises of the Lord's healing. I encouraged him to lay hands on his wife and believe God for a miracle. From God's answer to both of our prayers, we both were assured that we had met under divine appointment, not only for companionship in flight but also for his wife's healing.

God's provision was abundant! This Christian spoke Spanish and was able to assist me through customs. We did not exchange names or addresses, but I would love to know the rest of the story about his wife.

When I arrived, I also became a recipient of the wonderful hospitality from the Manning family for almost a week, until Isaac got the old, abandoned mission van to work. Because it had sat idle for some time, rust had accumulated in the radiator. When he determined the van had been adequately repaired, we packed it to capacity and started south for Rosanna and Isaac's new assignment.

We drove for hours over rugged mountains and winding roads. Finally everything started to look alike to me. Eerie feelings swept over me as we came to the many checkpoints along the way. Armed soldiers checked the vehicles for weapons on their way to El Salvador's revolution.

We arrived safely in San Marcos by late afternoon and began to unpack. The year-old house rented for them by the church men was still unfinished. There was a roof but no ceilings, and the eaves were still open. This gave the winds, insects, and birds free course to enter the house. There were glass window panes on the north and east sides of the house. In the back shuttered window openings were used, which opened onto a mix of coffee bushes, banana, and other tropical trees.

The first morning we awakened to the crowing of roosters and a clucking hen with her brood of chicks. She was industriously scratching through the debris of garbage left by the former tenants to find food for her little flock of ten chicks. As I scanned the house and yard, there was no doubt in my mind that there would be plenty to do for quite some time.

The people in this old Spanish town were very friendly. However, there were a few who watched us with suspicion as if to say, "What are you doing here?" San Marcos and the surrounding area had a population of approximately 2,000. In this region there was little communication with the outside world, for there was no airstrip, no telephones, and no two-way radio communication system.

There was electricity and water for several hours of the day. Before drinking, the water needed to be boiled and strained through a filtering crock. We were thankful for our old Maytag washing machine. Clothes were hung on strings stretched throughout the house for drying.

Since there was no church building here, a house had been purchased to remodel for a sanctuary. That first week Isaac helped the men to tear out partitions and pour hand-mixed concrete. The men were excited, for God had answered their prayers for a missionary couple, and soon a church for worship would be a reality.

By the second week the foreboding clouds of a tropical storm hung heavy above us. The storm was pressing down hard over Mexico; and we were receiving the tail end of it, which brought us rain and cold, damp temperatures. In spite of Isaac's diligent efforts to close the eaves with cardboard from our packing boxes, Rosanna came down with a heavy cold. We lined Nathaniel's crib and topped it with a blanket to ward off the chilling drafts.

There were millions of swarming mosquitoes, and we were warned to watch for scorpions in the house. A scorpion sting can be fatal to a small child or to an adult who is allergic to bee stings. The promises of Psalm 91 became a part of our daily life as we sought God's protection from the many dangers.

On Friday night we gathered for Bible study in a brown adobe house at the top of the hill. Although these people were not Christians, they were eager to hear the gospel. With the tropical storm past, the night air was hot and sultry. Women and men from the community filled the house to capacity. They sat attentively as Isaac shared from the Scriptures, even though many of them were seated on the floor. Isaac presented an edifying message and urged them to give their hearts to the Lord.

Isaac and Rosanna were the first Mennonite missionaries assigned to this area. There were six other small house-churches associated with this group of believers. It was difficult and time-consuming for a minister to reach these groups. Even horses could not travel to one of the areas because of the steep terrain. Rosanna and Isaac desired to minister to those in these remote areas of Honduras and possibly over the border in El Salvador.

By the time we had finished unpacking, Rosanna began to have back pain. Sometimes she was unable to walk or handle the baby. As a nurse, she realized she needed medical attention. The van's tank was all but empty of gasoline, and the town's only gas station had been without gas for several weeks. We prayed earnestly for a miracle of healing, and the people of the church came to have an anointing service. Our efforts seemed to be in vain, for nothing was happening to improve her condition.

We had many questions for the Lord: Was this the work of satan to destroy their ministry? Was it not God who had led them to this place? The fields were white unto harvest. Before they moved here, the church members had prayed long hours into the night for a missionary couple to bring revival to the community. The hunger in the hearts of these people for a better way of life was evident everywhere we went.

For two long weeks we waited and prayed for understanding of what was taking place in our lives. Our minds and bodies were taxed. I sometimes felt I had very little strength left after baking bread, tending the baby, caring for Rosanna, cooking, doing laundry, and purifying our daily supply of water.

One morning I especially needed to get away from it all. I could not speak the language and was sure I would get lost if I walked far from the house, for every house on every street looked exactly alike. Gray adobe houses began to appear more dismal each time I looked up the street. Although I could only say "good morning and thank you" in Spanish and was reluctant to go out, I decided to walk down the street a few doors to a local store. I sat on a stool there and gave everyone a cheerful good morning smile, hoping that someone would discern my need for friendship. After five minutes, however, I ascertained my body language and gestures confused them and decided to give up.

Those nights held long hours of prayerful pleas as I lay sleepless for hours on end until I fell asleep from pure exhaustion. Yet I would be awakened soon after as the town dogs were disturbed by the men of the town scuffling home from the taverns. The dogs' shrill barks resounded through the stillness of the night.

It was election time in the country, which meant that campesinos, or country men, would also come to party in the town. They had celebrations with firecrackers throughout the night. The firecrackers exploded not far from my half shuttered window, sometimes hissing with a final "puff-puff" through the dried banana leaves in our courtyard. Over and over I quoted the Scripture from Second Timothy 1:7, "For God hath not given us the spirit of fear; but of power, and of love, and of a sound mind."

I was concerned for the baby as I tended him at night and was careful to tuck the mosquito netting around the crib so that a scorpion could not get to him. I found it virtually impossible to rest in the peace of Jesus.

One morning just before dawn as I was praying, I heard the rapid succession of gunfire in the distance. I was petrified with the horrible thought that someone had been placed before a firing squad. Only a river divided San Marcos from El Salvador.

God is always faithful even though at times we may have to wait to understand His plan. I prayed for added strength as I began to repack barrels for leaving. Much of this work fell to me since Isaac had business matters to attend to with the church. We earnestly asked God to send gasoline to the town so that we could get Rosanna to the city for medical attention.

Although he had written, I had no word from Paul, for the mail was slow and unpredictable. Each day I anticipated the toot-toot of the mailman's bicycle horn only to be disappointed. We had been at this place for only a month, but to me it seemed so much longer.

After three days Isaac said, "I feel there will be gasoline at the station this morning; today we will leave." We took our clothes, a crib and rocking chair, and gathered all our pillows to pack around Rosanna for support. As we approached the gas station, we saw the gasoline truck was there and just starting to unload the gasoline. Glory to God for this perfect timing!

The Manning family welcomed us with concern and love once again. The doctors diagnosed Rosanna's problem as a compression fracture of the back and advised that we return to the States immediately for better x-rays and medical attention.

I called home and informed Paul what had taken place and to change the luggage he was bringing since the children would be coming back with us as soon as a birth certificate and passport papers could be secured for Nathaniel. When Paul arrived, he and Isaac drove to the capital in Tegucigalpa to get these documents so that we could bring the baby out of the country. Under ordinary conditions this could take months. However, God worked on some hearts and the papers were given without the usual bribes or favors.

From here, they traveled to San Marcos to bring out the rest of the possessions we had left behind. While cleaning up, they discovered a scorpion just over the six-foot partition next to Nathaniel's crib. We praise God for this protection.

The Sunday before leaving the Manning's home, we drove up to a high hill overlooking the city. Even though Rosanna was in pain, she also needed this ride. We got out of the van and stood overlooking the city. There were no words—only tears, tears of grief as Rosanna and Isaac saw the spiritual reality of a harvest they could not glean. I also wept, for I felt their hearts were broken and bleeding for these needy people. It was also our dream to witness an outpouring of God's Holy Spirit here as we had experienced in Tocoa. Yet we have a faithful Father who knows best, and He poured in the oil of consolation.

The five of us arrived back in the United States on May 21. About a month later, Isaac received a letter from the church people of San Marcos stating that more than 300 persons had been killed near the town of San Marcos as they tried to escape into San Marcos across the river. The revolution in El Salvador had become a full-blown war. I had indeed heard persons being shot. The men at the church were now required to minister to the refugees and had little time to devote to the work of the church.

The children stayed with us until Rosanna received healing for her back. Then they moved back into their own home. This was a difficult chapter in our life. However, we experienced much of our heavenly Father's faithfulness through it all.

Chapter 21

Hearts Braided With Love

All true love demands the sacrifice of one's personal desires and ambitions, whether it is in a family or a spiritual relationship. Our heavenly Father gave His only Son Jesus that we might be redeemed and adopted into the family of God. God is love, and as children of God, our relationships built on Christ will naturally be sacrificial as circumstances demand.

I think of that love as strands braided together—with the Lord, my husband, and our children—to make one strong cord. This makes for a stronger witness, greater ministry, more joy, and multiplied thanksgiving. I pray that God is being glorified through the braiding of love found in the united ministry outreach of our family.

Many chapters could be written on the blessed opportunities that were ours to be behind the "Anvil of God's Word." Often it was one-to-one ministry, sitting down to counsel with an open Bible as we endeavored to lead someone to a better life in Jesus. Others needed comfort from a broken heart or wounded spirit. We have led small Bible studies for persons who wanted to move into greater maturity in their Christian life. And we have been blessed with opportunities to share our testimony of the Lord's greatness with little country churches and with big churches in town.

I will never forget one huge cathedral-like sanctuary with its towering ceiling. I was shocked to hear the echo of my own voice while I shared what the Lord had done in our lives. I am often awed that the Holy Spirit provides us with the stamina, courage, and anointing for so many varied circumstances.

On one of these occasions, I was praying for a message that would meet the needs of a particular congregation. I wanted them to know it was fresh from heaven. In the heading of my Bible in the Book of James, I have drawn a picture of what I was given in a dream that night after prayer. I saw a gigantic tree that reached from earth to Heaven. It was growing in the midst of the church parking lot. The tree was heavily laden with massive fruits of many varieties, colors, and shapes. Some of the fruit was past harvesting and had fallen to the ground. No one seemed to be aware of the tree's existence as they walked by.

I thought, *What a terrible waste!* The following day I was contemplating the meaning of the dream and asked the Holy Spirit to reveal the interpretation. The Holy Spirit directed me to read James 1. In the seventeenth verse, a revelation illuminated my understanding: "Every good gift and every perfect gift is from above, and cometh down from the Father of lights, with whom is no variableness, neither shadow of turning."

Now I understood more fully. The fruit represented gifts He has provided for us to use in ministry and are accessible to us as believers. The heavenly Father has provided what we need in the nine gifts of the Spirit recorded in First Corinthians 12:4-11.

Now there are diversities of gifts, but the same Spirit. And there are differences of administrations, but the same Lord. And there are diversities of operations, but it is the same God which worketh all in all. But the manifestation of the Spirit is given to every man to profit withal. For to one is given by the Spirit the word of wisdom; to another the word of knowledge by the same Spirit; to another faith by the same Spirit; to another the gifts of healing by the same Spirit; to another the working of miracles; to another prophecy; to another discerning of spirits; to another divers kinds of tongues; to another the interpretation of tongues: but all these worketh that one and the selfsame Spirit, dividing to every man severally as He will.

There are different gifts for the various circumstances needed in serving. We will realize the availability of these gifts as we commit ourselves wholly unto Him.

I am thankful for the provision of an ongoing salvation: the gift of faith the unbeliever cannot understand, or the anointing of the Holy Spirit that equips us with gifts for ministry. We must use and activate these inherited blessings, so we can become an extension of Jesus Christ's ministry. The nine gifts are given for ministry, while the fruit of the Spirit—love, joy, peace, longsuffering, gentleness, goodness, faith, meekness, temperance—is developed (see Gal. 5:22-23). The nine gifts of the Spirit are not for a select few, but for Christians who want to serve the Lord.

The test of Christian obedience to the Father is found in the Book of James:

But be ye doers of the word, and not hearers only, deceiving your own selves. For if any be a hearer of the word, and not a doer, he is like unto a man beholding his natural face in a glass: for he beholdeth himself, and goeth his way, and straightway forgetteth what manner of man he was. But whoso looketh into the perfect law of liberty, and continueth therein, he being not a forgetful hearer, but a doer of the work, this man shall be blessed in his deed (James 1:22-25).

What I saw in the visionary dream were gifts to be used for ministry in the harvest fields of the Lord's vineyard. I have to ask myself, *Have I always used His full provision for the harvest fields in my life?*

By the summer of 1980, the atmosphere of our home was relaxed and pleasurable as we enjoyed having the children close by once again. However, in late August I had a new test of faith. I found how closely my mother-heart was braided with love for my son and his family one evening when they surprised us by sharing their call from God to help with a church-planting work in Maine.

Until this time the Church of the Brethren had no congregations north of Brooklyn, New York. Some men from the Atlantic
Northeast District had a vision to start a work in the New England
states. This proposed mission had been presented at our official
board meeting in March with a call for some couples to volunteer
to start this mission project.

I had already discovered that being a missionary's mother was
far more than could be seen on the surface. The sacrifice of having
part of our family in Honduras for several years taught me much
about intercession for their safety. Hours were spent in spiritual
warfare against the forces of evil that raged to destroy them and
their ministry. All this can be tiring and time-consuming. I spent
many nights wondering if all was well, and there were times when
my heart was aching with my longing to see them. Even those
longed-for letters came only after two to four weeks of waiting and
many trips to the mailbox.

I had difficulty sitting down to a table spread with a feast of
good things knowing that their fare would be meager and their fellowship with other believers minimal. Often I was too weary with
intercession to perform my general housework when I sensed in
my spirit they were facing a crisis. At times I found comfort and
strength from our friends, John and Reba Hershey, who were in
tune with the Holy Spirit and who also sensed these moments of
crisis and prayed for them. The Hershey's often followed up several weeks afterward with a call to see what we had heard about
the children, for they knew we would probably have a letter telling
of some definite danger or trouble they had faced at that particular
time. What a gift from God to have such intimate friends!

I was struggling to forget the unpleasant experiences of San
Marcos. The stress of these traumatic days had a physical effect on
my heart. My soul was in turmoil. I wanted Shannon and Marian to
be obedient to God's call to service, yet my heart ached to think of
the sacrifice. God had not prepared my heart for Shannon's call as
in Rosanna's life. As grandparents we would not see our grandsons

often, for the trip would take 12 hours of travel. For several days I struggled with the weight of the matter until I knew I needed to get away from home to a place where I could sort out my emotions.

Paul and I drove to Yorktown, Virginia for a few days. We got a motel room along the ocean, sat in silence, held hands, prayed together, walked on the beach, and spent hours sitting on our balcony watching the waves. I needed to make a choice. I could either fight the waves in my life, only to drown in my own self-pity and despair, or I could choose to ride my waves like a surfer and enjoy being lifted to new heights of inner peace. I began to gratefully reflect on God's goodness. How blessed we were to have children who were not only called of God but chosen for special ministry!

The Lord gave me a Scripture that gave me added strength and understanding:

> *Is not this the fast that I have chosen? to loose the bands of wickedness, to undo the heavy burdens, and to let the oppressed go free, and that ye break every yoke? Is it not to deal thy bread to the hungry, and that thou bring the poor that are cast out to thy house? when thou seest the naked, that thou cover him; and that thou hide not thyself from thine own flesh? Then shall thy light break forth as the morning, and thine health shall spring forth speedily: and thy righteousness shall go before thee; the glory of the Lord shall be thy rereward. Then shalt thou call, and the Lord shall answer; thou shalt cry, and He shall say, Here I am. If thou take away from the midst of thee the yoke, the putting forth of the finger, and speaking vanity; and if thou draw out thy soul to the hungry, and satisfy the afflicted soul; then shall thy light arise in obscurity, and thy darkness be as the noonday: and the Lord shall guide thee continually, and satisfy thy soul in drought, and make fat thy bones: and thou shalt be like a watered garden, and like a spring of water, whose waters fail not. And **they that shall be of thee** shall build the old waste places: thou shalt raise up the foundations of many generations; and thou shalt be called,*

*The repairer of the breach, The restorer of paths to dwell
in. ... **Then shalt thou delight thyself in the Lord; and I
will cause thee to ride upon the high places of the earth**...*
(Isaiah 58:6-12,14).

This Scripture has been such a blessing through the years when
I have become lonely, weary, and discouraged. God is so wonderful to reveal Himself as fresh manna in this present age. I praise
the Lord that He helped me find victory over my fleshly heart's desires. It has not always been easy to have many miles separate us
from loved ones. However, I am grateful I can say that no time or
distance can unbraid the cords of love that bind us together in the
love of Christ Jesus.

It was difficult for Shannon and Marian that I did not exuberantly accept their call to missions. But as their years of parenting
have developed more fully, I believe they now understand my
struggle. Shannon had helped with the farming. He had been there
through those crucial times of his father's illness. When they left
the farm and moved near us, we could travel to visit them in a few
minutes. Until their call to serve in Maine, I was not aware how
much I had grown to depend on Shannon and the comfort and security that nearness brought. My selfish thoughts needed to bow to
God's call to their harvest field.

In February 1981, we kept the boys so that they could travel to
Maine to look over the community of Lewiston. This was the proposed area for the mission. In April they returned to Maine to look
for a house.

There were six couples from Lancaster, Lebanon, and Franklin Counties who responded to the call for this church-planting
work. The commissioning service for these families was held on
May 31, 1981.

In June, Shannon was afflicted with something unusual in his
feet and legs. Some days it made it virtually impossible for him to
walk. He lost three months work from his job. We wondered if this
were a detour from the Lord or a roadblock from satan? Because

of this illness, Shannon and Marian were unable to leave for Maine with the other couples.

By January, his condition had improved, and their spirits were undaunted by this test of faith. February 3, 1983, our driveway as well as the highways were covered with a sheet of ice, but Shannon and Marian finished loading the U-Haul to leave for Maine. Joy radiated from their faces, although they felt traces of sadness at leaving us behind. The day they had dreamed of for almost two years had finally arrived, and they were not going to let this wintry morning hold them back.

For their first year in Maine, church services were held in the basement of a fish market. What an unusual place for these "fishers of men." Later they were able to lease a Jewish synagogue, which they bought a year later. The Jewish congregation had built a new 1.5 million dollar edifice. With some minor renovations, this brick building has proven to be an ample and lovely church for the Lewiston Church of the Brethren.

In May, we traveled to Maine to visit the children. Their house was always a veritable depot of action, which Shannon jokingly renamed from 10-3 Hillview to 10-3 Hillzoo. However, they were able to touch many children's lives in that place with the love of Christ. Out of some 90 apartments in the complex at Hillview, there were only seven fathers. Consequently, Shannon became a caring father image for many young boys and girls. They would come to play games in the evenings and on weekends, and they often ended up sitting on his knee sharing their troubles and listening to his stories about Jesus.

During Shannon and Marian's year at Hillview, they sought the Lord's direction about making this their permanent home. When they were convinced they were to continue the work with the church in Maine, they bought a house in the city of Auburn. They returned for their furniture that had been stored in Pennsylvania, finished up some business affairs, and headed north once again.

Auburn and Lewiston are twin cities, divided by a river. God blessed them with a house situated in a nice residential section of Auburn. It is constructed of cedar shingles painted a soft gray with pink trim and shutters. It becomes beautifully framed in a setting of snow! Their home is nestled in a cove with a woods. Trees of oak, ash, white birch, hemlock, and white pine surround the house. The house is adequate and convenient for them and guests. Many have enjoyed their warm hospitality as they traveled from Pennsylvania and other parts of the country to view the mission. Winter snows make it a veritable winter wonderland. Our grandsons enjoy sledding, tobogganing, and skiing on slopes that are within a few miles of their home.

We believe God guided them to this quiet part of the city. Two years before they bought the house, the Lord told Shannon that their property would have a stone wall and a stream. A stone retaining wall stands along their current driveway, and a stream runs through the property. God has been so good to our family through His direction and confirmation.

The predominantly French Catholic background of many people of the community varies considerably from the conservative Anabaptist views of the Church of the Brethren. However, the church at Lewiston continues to grow. New congregations have been established in Brunswick and Gardners. The Lewiston congregation opened the Lewiston Area Missions School in 1994.

Marvin, Darrell, and Lee were enrolled at the Lisbon Falls Christian Academy. Each of the boys had newspaper routes as soon as they were old enough to accept the responsibility. According to weather conditions, they faithfully covered their routes by riding their bikes, walking, or pulling a sled. They learned to brave the darkness and endure below zero temperatures. Their small businesses became a source of pride and a responsible outlook toward financial planning.

Their dependability on the paper routes opened other opportunities for employment in the neighborhood as they grew older. As teens, these jobs ranged from caring for lawns, shoveling snow, painting houses and garages to mason tending. Marvin's competency opened the way for Darrell, who in turn paved the way for Lee, as they moved into adult employment after graduation.

Most years we have made an annual trip to Maine, usually near Christmas. Then Shannon's family usually comes back to Pennsylvania for a week in the summer. These regular six-month visits make our separation more endurable. By traveling in December, we sometimes encounter snow or icy highways. During one trip, we encountered snow in Portland underneath a clear, full moon. The farther north we drove, the deeper the snow became. We were excited that we would soon be seeing our family, and the snow added a special touch to the Christmas spirit as we played carols on the tapedeck. The silent blanket of white was reminiscent of the sensation and quietness of a sleigh ride. We thrilled over the majestic beauty during the next 40 miles of our trip as the tree branches bowed low in the moonlight frosted by sparkling, crystal flakes. There were few houses in this area, just mile after mile of stately pines now laden with the heavy snowfall.

Shannon always enjoyed the beauty of winter snows. When on the farms, we lived in an area where winds swept down over the mountains onto our flat, fertile fields creating much drifting snow. One particularly bad storm was frightening! We had young cattle at the second farm, which was a field's length from our place. These heifers needed care each day to be sure that their water cups had not frozen and that they had feed and bedding. This was Shannon's responsibility. After he had left to do this chore, a fierce wind began to blow, reducing visibility to zero. Paul came in from the barn to call Bill Pryor, who lived at the other farm, and asked him to tell Shannon to stay with them until the winds subsided. Bill had trouble getting to the barn. Shannon was not to be found. Though only 16, Shannon realized the seriousness of the situation and the possibility of losing his way. He traveled home from the barn by holding to the fence of the barnyard until he reached the field fence. Then followed this fence and then another until he reached the one that came next to our house. This meant he had a greater distance to travel, but it was the only way he felt he would not get lost in the storm. When he finally came up over the porch and into the house, we saw at once that his face was frostbitten. We were definitely snowbound, but this was a matter that demanded immediate first aid. I flipped open my first aid book for instructions on frostbite, as Paul was helping him out of his snow plastered and frozen clothes. It was a frightening experience that left no visible scars, but I still bless God for keeping him safe in that wildest of blizzards.

One of the compensations of Shannon and Marian's work in Maine is the many snow experiences that they have enjoyed. In the winter, Shannon is on call for snow removal and plowing for the city housing authority.

We are grateful that our son and his wife have chosen to serve the Lord instead of pursuing the riches of this world. It has meant sacrifice of family, personal comfort, and pleasures. Yet they receive special rewards that compensate for these sacrifices as they serve in the office of deacon, Sunday school superintendent, youth director, and last but not necessarily least, janitor of the church. Both Shannon and Marian have spent innumerable hours in Bible teaching, disciplining, counseling, and visitation. Many times they have ministered into the wee hours of the morning. Shannon accompanies the pastor on evangelistic visitation and assists with anointings and deliverance ministry that are needed. Eventually Marvin and his wife Ruby took over the janitorial responsibilities of the church.

Marian is gifted in administration and has been a real help with organization of Sunday school, vacation Bible school, and Women's Bible Hour. She mentored many women through physical, emotional, and marital problems. She enjoys planning church and school social functions. Her gift of hospitality requires many hours of planning and work.

As I view this work, I can see the fulfillment of Isaiah 58:12, for they are building up the old waste places, raising up the foundations of generations, repairing the breach, and restoring paths to dwell in. We give glory to God for His love and faithfulness to us as a family. We delight in Him as we serve, for it does cause us to ride the high places of the earth with joy and satisfaction in the Holy Ghost.

The children remember us with cards on special days and occasions, even with their busy schedules. Several years ago Shannon surprised us with letters of tribute on Mother's and Father's Days. I am sure he spent hours in contemplation, for writing does not come easy to him. We considered his letters a rich and rare treasure. I share my letter so you may see the special braiding of love between our hearts.

May 1990

Dear Mother:

James 4:14 says, "Life is but a vapor, how quickly it passes through our fingers." I was made to realize this even more several weeks ago when visiting Upton church. I looked into the familiar faces of the youth, and then realized that they were not my friends, but my friends' children.

I realize it because my oldest is about to graduate and start a life of his own. I realize it when summer and winter blend together and soon a year passes, and it seems only a month.

I realize it when my baby sister is 30 and I am 40. I realize it because I have been married 20 years, which means I have been away from home as long as at home.

This is not to make you or me sad, because it is truly a blessing. God has given us this blessing of life and the rich things we've both had to experience. But it does bring me to the realization that there are many things I want to thank you for. Many of which may seem small, but oftentimes the biggest lessons are learned by the small things.

Thank you, Mother, for your part in bringing me into the world. I understand it was not an easy experience, nor were the complications that followed.

Thanks for the things I can't remember that you did while caring for me as a baby—in all the ways that were not so pleasant—and for teaching me to walk and talk, and for watching that I didn't get hurt or lost when I crawled through the hole in the fence.

Thanks for teaching me the beauty of nature, whether in the clouds of the sky, the smell of a rose, or in the little caterpillars that I used to enjoy playing with. God's creation has become an important part of my life, of which I am sure I can attribute to your teaching.

Thank you for accepting with joy all the bouquets of dandelions I picked for you, even though you knew they would only last for a few hours. This taught me the joy of giving.

Thank you for teaching me not to cry wolf, when I fell from the swing set and you didn't respond. You were being a good mother and I knew it then too.

Thank you for not giving in when I threw a temper tantrum. That taught me that your word was final.

Thanks for bundling me up to play in the snow. (Many have never learned the beauty of the cold and the snow.)

I remember the time you came into my bedroom singing a Christmas song and ringing a string of bells. How young and excited you looked! You taught me the excitement of holidays.

Thank you for forcing me to weed the garden, although I hated it, it taught me to work.

I thank you for the many, many times you nursed me back to health during a time of high fever or croup; for carrying the fear of we children contacting polio in the late 50's; and for all the nightmares you somehow got me through.

Thanks for all the effort you put forth in getting me through school. No project was too large or small, or time-consuming for you to help with. Remember the clown suit for the first grade, the Indian tepee for the fourth, and my fifth grade teacher? Oh dear!!

Thanks for not buying $.39 cereal when $.29 cereal could be bought or buying a watermelon if they were over $1.59. This taught me to be thrifty with my money.

Thank you for teaching me to be honest no matter what the price.

Thanks, Mother, for all the seemingly unnoticed mundane tasks of a mother, such as washing, ironing, cooking, cleaning, etc., which I never heard you complain about.

Thanks for all the effort you put forth to involve me in 4-H Club and F.F.A. The endless trips to meetings, to the fair, to the corn patch then to town to sell corn, and pushing me to achieve. These were all ways to build character and gave me experience to build on later in life.

Thanks for teaching me the things I don't know how I learned—like knowing right from wrong, the importance of being truthful in all things, knowing how to respect a woman and not misuse or abuse anyone, how to sense when someone is in need or hurting, and the beauty of minute details.

And most of all I appreciate the spiritual training you gave me, whether it was reading Bible stories or volunteering your services at church. This was the foundation of my faith.

Thanks for getting me through the dating years, whether by giving advice, pressing my shirts, helping me buy a corsage, or having a sandwich ready when I would fly through the kitchen. This yielded me a priceless wife and a good life.

Thanks for your concern for me when I was late, even though I didn't fully understand it then.

Thanks for the magazine article you gave me on my wedding day. I've read it many times since.

And thank you for the thousand other things that I haven't written that will remain part of my memory for the rest of my life.

Although I have been away for 20 years now, I am thankful for your constant concern and prayer support as you and Dad have stood back of us in our ministry in Maine. I know it has not always been easy for you. However, as I rub shoulders with those who have had difficult childhood experiences, I am constantly reminded what a rich heritage I have had. I owe that heritage to you, Mother and Dad.

Thank you for being the best mother in the world!

Happy Mother's Day
Love,
Your son, Shannon

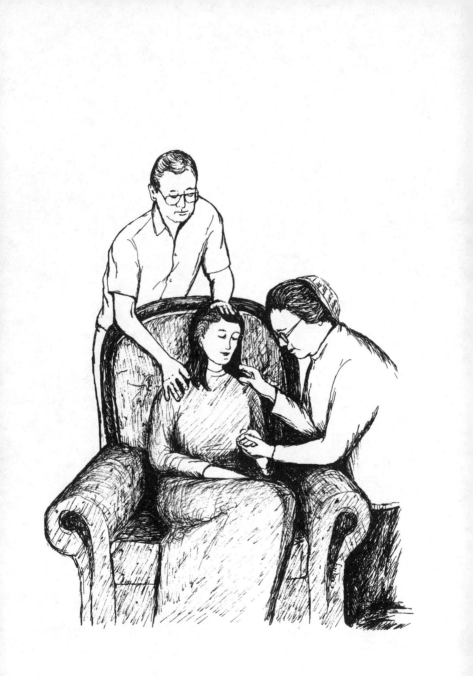

Chapter 22

Freely Ye Have Received—Freely Give

We have been blessed to be a blessing to others, and our "family of God" continues to grow through ministry. For more than 20 years we struggled in self-initiated effort to serve the Lord with little power and minimal fruit. Since receiving the Second Blessing (baptism of the Holy Spirit), and the anointing that accompanies that personal Pentecost, we regret those wasted years.

At last we know the truth, and the truth has set us free to enjoy the fulfillment of being Christ's servants. For more than two decades now, the Lord has satisfied the longings of our heart as we continue to accept opportunities to teach His Word through workshops, retreats, and mission weekends. It is humbling to experience God's love so freely bestowed. How indebted we feel to Him! Paul has always been an encouragement to me, whether we minister separately or as a team. We are yoked together for outreach ministry in the renewal of the Holy Spirit. We know that all glory and praise is His and His alone, for freely we have received and freely we desire to give (see Mt. 10:8b).

These blessings had a price tag. When illness required us to sell our farms, Paul was no longer self-employed. After his healing, God provided jobs, but they were not high-paying ones. However, we have learned the rich reward of spirituality that reaches into a realm of satisfaction money could never provide. Some persons who had prayed for Paul's healing actually persecuted us because they could not perceive that the baptism of the Holy Spirit we received at the same time was an added blessing of God's marvelous grace. At times we felt lonely, misunderstood, and set apart. Consequently, this only drove us to the secret place of prayer for communion with our all-knowing God.

We read what the apostle Paul wrote about ministry:

> *We then, as workers together with Him, beseech you also that ye receive not the grace of God in vain. ... But in all things approving ourselves as the ministers of God, in much patience, in afflictions, in necessities, in distresses, in stripes, in imprisonments, in tumults, in labours, in watchings, in fastings; by pureness, by knowledge, by longsuffering, by kindness, by the Holy Ghost, by love unfeigned, by the word of truth, by the power of God, by the armour of righteousness on the right hand and on the left, by honour and dishonour, by evil report and good report: as deceivers, and yet true; as unknown; and yet well known; as dying, and, behold, we live; as chastened, and not killed; as sorrowful, yet always rejoicing; as poor, yet making many rich; as having nothing, and yet possessing all things* (2 Corinthians 6:1,4-10).

Stephen Burkholder was born April 19, 1983. Rosanna returned to nursing soon afterward. They felt an urgency to gather funds for Isaac's Bible college and seminary education so that they would be better equipped to continue their ministry.

One day while babysitting Stephen, I had a frightening experience. At this time he was still drinking his mother's milk. Feeling concerned that milk she left with me might not always be sufficient for the day, she purchased a milk formula for an emergency backup. One particular day, I found I had a defective plastic bottle liner and needed more milk for his afternoon feeding, so I made a half-and-half mixture with the bought formula. As soon as the milk hit his stomach, he vomited violently.

In a few minutes his eyes were swollen shut, and his fingers and ears were swelled until they stuck out. Because I knew the swelling could cut off his breathing, I called the hospital where Rosanna worked for instructions. She told me to head for the doctor's office and she would meet us there. This was a 14-mile drive, but was closer than the hospital. It was a wild ride as I flew around the curves and over the hills, occasionally reaching over with one hand to see if Stephen was still breathing. Thanks to the Lord, we made it!

Dr. David Hess, a man of 70, who has delivered and doctored hundreds of babies, said this was the most violent reaction to milk that he had ever seen in his many years of practice. By the time we reached the office, the worst was past. Had he not vomited, I am sure Stephen would not have survived. After this, any food product with milk was carefully kept from his diet. When he was a year old and getting into things, he picked up an empty milk carton and put it to his face. This caused an immediate rash.

In August of that year, Isaac and Rosanna moved to Honeye, New York, where Isaac enrolled in Elim Bible Institute. Several days before graduation, the students have a special time of prayer and fasting for future guidance. During this time one of the students had a vision for Isaac and Rosanna. In the vision he saw them ministering in a city surrounded by high mountains. They tucked this away in their minds for future confirmation.

In the summer of 1986 Stephen came to his mother one day and said, "Mamma, pour me a glass of milk. God just told me I can drink milk." What a test of faith! As Rosanna surveyed the unusual expression and the joy on his little three-year-old face, she had to believe that he had indeed heard the voice of God. She poured a little in a glass. He drank it and nothing happened. Then he said, "Please pour me some more." She poured him a full glass of milk, and he drank it with no harmful reaction, not even a rash. What a powerful demonstration of God's love!

Each season affords new challenges. There are the mother-daughter banquets, father-son banquets, Christmas and Easter chalk talks, evangelistic campaigns in the winter months and Lay

Renewal weekends. New challenges press us more deeply into the Word, and we also learn and grow as we serve others. During these times, we rely on the Holy Spirit to give direction as we listen to those who come to our house for prayer. We often weep with them as they agonize over heart-wrenching experiences. I once saw a sign by the side of the road that I liked, "Empathy is your pain in my heart." I never apologize for tears, for they are a language in themselves. Jesus wept, why should we not also have this kind of compassion for one another?

Paul was asked to teach a weekly home Bible study for a group of people in the Lemasters area. They wanted to learn more of God's Word and requested a study on the parables of Jesus and the prophet Isaiah. This study met within view of our old homestead. One fall night during a full moon, we were sitting in session when something happened deep in my spirit. The house and barn to the east became silhouetted in the moonlight against the black sky. Here was the place where we planted seeds in the soil; now within view of these same acres, we were asked to plant seeds in the hearts of women and men.

These days in which we live are filled with evil, and I encourage you, if you have never received this baptism of the Holy Ghost for witnessing power, go to your prayer closet and ask. Luke 11:13 tells us, "If ye then, being evil, know how to give good gifts unto your children: how much more shall your heavenly Father give the Holy Spirit to them that ask Him?"

Those in ministry need to be refreshed from time to time. We needed to spend time with brothers and sisters who have also received this gift of the Holy Spirit. We found this refreshing fellowship in the monthly meetings of the Full Gospel Business Men's Fellowship International. Each month a guest speaker would share the transformation of his life under the "second work of grace." Women's Aglow International has also been a great blessing to me. Both of these organizations do not take the place of the church. They encourage members to be edified and work actively in their own churches to inspire and edify their brothers and sisters and to reach out to the unsaved and hurting of their communities. Paul and I have served on the boards of these organizations as well as speaking for many chapters. These are non-denominational ministries and have brought thousands into the church who would never have darkened the door of a church.

Revival services have always been another source of refreshment. On one of these occasions, we visited the Shady Pine Mennonite Church to hear the evangelist Ramsumair Harry. Brother Harry was born in the West Indies to a Hindu family. Upon his conversion to Christianity, he was considered dead by his family. They conducted a funeral for him to signify he was disowned and cut off from his earthly family.

That night after his sermon, he gave an altar call. During this time God gave me a vision of a toy box. I looked at the toy box with wonderment. The head of an E.T. toy began to rise from the midst of the dolls, balls, tractors, and other toys. Because I thought this was something the Lord wanted me to share with the minister, I went forward and whispered the vision to him. He shared the vision with the congregation, and several parents responded by saying that they had bought these toys for their children. The evangelist admonished the parents to go home and check their children's toys and pray for the Holy Spirit to give them discernment to determine which ones were demonic inspired.

I have witnessed that persons who have experienced the baptism of the Holy Spirit are more discerning of satan's tactics. Rightly so, for one of the gifts promised is the "gift of discernment." These gifts of the Holy Spirit do not make us more holy or righteous, but they are still invaluable. Through them we receive warnings for our protection and greater victory in combating the evil forces in our lives.

One lovely spring afternoon in May, Katrina and William Reighard shared their plans to be married on August 17, 1985. We believe the Lord brought them together, for Bill is a fine Christian man from Woodbury, Pennsylvania. He had graduated from Penn State University and was working with Pennzoil Oil Company. His company was sending him to Long Island, and they decided it would be wise to go together. At this time Katrina had worked as program director for several summers at our church camp. Prior to this she worked at our local Christian camp, Camp Joy-El.

She enjoyed helping to make a difference in the lives of youth. Camp Eder broadened this experience and provided her with opportunity to encourage many to make decisions to accept Christ. She counseled many who were struggling with problems in their lives due to broken homes, sex, and drugs.

Because Katrina is a nature lover, she decided to have her wedding by the stream at Camp Eder. This lovely spot is covered with nature's carpet of soft, velvety green moss. For those who are in love with God's great outdoors, it was truly a picturesque spot for Katrina and Bill to exchange their wedding vows before the Lord and some 70 guests.

She wore an ankle-length gown of white lace over taffeta. She complimented this with a picture hat, waist-length veil, and an arm bouquet of red roses. Bill wore a black satin-trimmed tuxedo. They were a strikingly handsome couple! Every detail of the wedding was casual, just as they wanted it to be—without pomp and fanfare.

After the ceremony, the guests followed the bridal party from this beautiful spot by walking through a white trellis, decorated with asparagus fern, white daisies, and baby's breath to the reception in the newly-built pavilion by the creek. Guests were seated at tables in front of a huge stone fireplace, which was decorated with swags of the same type of flowers. Centerpieces arranged in white antique ironstone pitchers filled with blue and purple Bachelor's Buttons and Babies Breath along with white and green lace tablecloths tranformed the picnic tables into elegant settings. It was a beautiful country wedding!

Chapter 23

Springtime in Chile

Our dream to visit Osvaldo and his family in Santiago, Chile became a reality in October, 1985. He had recently bought and remodeled a house. In his home were private guest quarters on the second floor that overlooked a manicured lawn ornamented with fruit trees, flowers, and shrubbery.

Eighteen years had passed since Osvaldo spent a year at our home as an exchange student under the American Field Service Program. We longed to meet his mamita (mother), his sister Ximena, his brother Ramon, and his family. During his stay with us he had also shown us photos of the picturesque ports of Valpraiso, Vina del Mar, and his hometown of Curico, and we desired to experience their beauty firsthand.

The overnight flight to Santiago was tiring. This was soon forgotten upon landing as we pushed along with the crowd through lines at the customs office. How excited we were to see Osvaldo waiting beyond the glass enclosure! And how proud he was of his family and home! Located in a residential section of Santiago, his house had a view of the Andes Mountains rising to meet the sky. The very tips of the mountains were still snow covered from the winter just past, for while it was autumn in Pennsylvania, it was springtime in Chile.

Maria Euguenia met us with open arms, and we were soon acquainted with the children: Paulina, Constanza, and little Sebastian. What beautiful children! Sebastian, who was just learning to walk, greeted us shyly. Paul captured the girls' hearts immediately. Because their grandfathers had both died before they were born, Paul quickly filled that role as he bounced them on his legs.

Everything was done to make us welcome and comfortable. The maids placed fresh flowers in our bedroom, where spring breezes rustled through chiffon curtains and strains of soft classical Spanish music floated up the open stairway. Maria Euguenia's mother, Mrs. Perez, and sister Gabriella came to visit. Knowing that cooking is one of my hobbies, the cook took great care in preparing their traditional Chilean dishes.

City traffic was terrific! In six-lane highways through the heart of the city, eight vehicles were often abreast, each vying to be first through the traffic signals. Street vendors held out balloons, flowers, or snack foods to cars stopped in traffic jams, while car horns continuously blared from short-tempered drivers.

Beautiful flower boxes accented tall apartment complexes. Dazzling varieties and colors of flowers, hanging vines, and foliage plants had a way of pulling one's eyes upward 20 or more stories to spots of beauty among the tons of concrete of the city streets.

During the first weekend in Chile, we drove 150 miles to Mamita's house in the country, where Osvaldo was born. It was a thrilling moment as we embraced, for it was now many years that we had known each other only by stories, photographs, and Osvaldo's conversation. Even though we could not communicate verbally, her warm, friendly personality spoke volumes to us as she welcomed us into her country home. She served us coffee as we conversed with Osvaldo, who translated our impressions of their country and the excitement of seeing her grandchildren.

Osvaldo had bought a house in Curico for his mother's retirement home when she is ready to leave her country place in Triaco. We had stopped there on our way to visit his brother Ramon and his family. We found Ramon to be very different from Osvaldo. Ramon is a tall, big-framed man who is a true country *wassel* (cowboy). He is the owner and overseer of many sheep, with a crew of cowboys to ride range with him. Each summer their large flocks of sheep pasture over hundreds of acres of valleys and ridges, grazing as they go. When the pasture becomes short, they are driven farther up the Andes Mountains near the Argentina border to pasture lands that belonged to their Grandfather Leyton.

Before coming to the United States, Osvaldo sometimes accompanied Ramon with this work when school was not in session. He enjoyed riding range with his older brother on his special horse and being a part of the great outdoors.

At the close of our short visit with Ramon, we were ushered to the back of the house to a storage room for a surprise. Ramon had killed and dressed a lamb from his flock, which was to be roasted on an open pit at Mamita's house later in the day in the celebration of our coming. This reminded us of the feasts prepared in Bible times for guests. That afternoon as we watched it being roasted over charcoal at the back of the house, and smelled the aroma of succulent lamb as it turned to a perfect brown, we were overcome with emotion. What a special privilege to experience love and friendship so far from our homeland! Mamita completed the dinner with a special homemade bread, which she baked in a bed of hot ashes, a salad of tomato and sweet onions tossed with an oil dressing, rice, and beans. The lamb was unforgettable, braised to perfection!

After lunch we had a family communion. This traditional ritual expressed our love for one another. A small, dried, hollowed-out gourd was used as a serving cup. The strong tea used for this communion was brewed over a charcoal burner in the sunroom. The piping hot tea was then poured into the cup and passed to each person in the circle for a sip. These were thoughtful, almost sacred moments as everyone sat in silence. We realized this was our formal induction into the Leyton family circle. Every member of the Leyton family was present for this communion. We felt highly honored and cherish this special occasion.

After a time of conversation, Mamita gave me a demonstration of spinning raw wool into fine thread on a simple wooden spool balanced in her lap. As her fingers deftly manipulated the thread around and around the twisting, wooden peg, she stated that such spinning will soon be a lost art in their country.

After dinner Osvaldo took us to the farm he owned, which was part of his inheritance from his grandfather. The long lane was lined on both sides with a wall of slender green trees. As we exited this wall of beauty, we saw a simple farmhouse and barn. Nearby, in a picturesque scene, were four wagon wheels leaning against a tree. They seemed to demand our attention and remind us of history past.

A few colorful chickens and a strutting, fan-tailed tom turkey welcomed us into the farmyard. Grandfather Leyton, now deceased, owned the adjoining farm. The stately hacienda with its long porch on two sides was graced with purple flowering vines that clung to the huge, round, white posts. At the entrance door of the house stood two four-foot clay pots, which once provided the family convenient access to water.

Mrs. Leyton, a step-grandmother, met us with a cordial Spanish greeting. Once again I was frustrated that I could not converse with her in her language, and I sensed she felt very much the same. She was a woman probably my own age with lines of determination showing in her countenance. Only a woman of much stamina could carry on the work around a farm like this.

On the east side of the rambling white house was an orchard long past its days of fruitfulness. Behind the orchard a field climbed the steep hillside. Dozens of goats were pasturing. It seemed as if we had stepped back in time as we thought of Grandfather Leyton and the happy times he shared with Ramon and Osvaldo and the goats on the hillside.

From what we were told, Grandfather Leyton was a full-blooded Spaniard and a proud one at that. For many years he had acquired his wealth through his cattle, both sheep and goats, on his thousands of acres of land and by harvesting grapes from his vineyards. Osvaldo shared with us that one day he gave up his will to live. His physician's efforts and Osvaldo's urgings could not persuade him differently, and his life was soon over.

After some time of conversation with interpretation, Mrs. Leyton excused herself. She went into the house a few moments and came back with a gift for us. She presented us with a most unique pelt of soft calf skin. This rug or wall hanging was made from a still-born calf. The hair was fine, soft, and spotted with brown and white. Osvaldo explained that this was the ultimate gift, a treasure shared by a farmer. We accepted it gratefully with the few words of thanksgiving we knew, "Gracias, Senora, Gracias!"

We returned to Mamita's for our final good-byes. Mamita was the caregiver for an aged great aunt, who lived in a building at the rear of her house. Her skin was wrinkled from her many years of life. No one, including herself, knew her age; but she looked as if she could be a hundred. She sat on a stool, and since it was Sunday, she held her open Bible in her lap. She was illiterate, for she had never had the opportunity to attend school. I sat down near her, and in my feeble efforts tried to express my love with touch. I patted her hands and caressed her face with my palms. I often think of her and her reverence for God's Word just by treasuring the open Bible. What a testimony of sincerity of her love and respect for the God she loved. I hope that I will know her in Glory when we both shall speak the same language.

I find it an embarrassment that here in America with all of our education and affluence, many desecrate our Sundays with labor, shopping, or whatever pleasures our hearts desire. The god of pleasure is robbing us of a clear-cut, precise testimony. God planned our rejuvenation on this day of worship and rest, for spirit, soul, and body.

I cherish the memory of Mamita's farewell gift of a bouquet of the most regal of all lilies, the pure, pristine, beautiful, white calla lilies from her garden.

We experienced so much in the first week of our vacation in Chile; how could the second one match it? Osvaldo, Paul, and I flew 750 miles south of Santiago, where we rented a car and drove to Puerto Monte, my favorite port city with boats, ships, horse-drawn carts, and open-air markets. From one of these markets, I was fortunate to purchase a large custom made rug woven by a famous and skilled elderly Indian woman from Easter Island. An ambassador from one of the countries of east Asia had ordered two identical rugs to take back to his country. However, when he wanted to return home, he had acquired too many treasures to be flown back and could only take one of them. The merchant told us about the rug, went to his house, and brought it for our inspection.

As we drove south on the Pan American Highway, we came to the German town of Fruitillar. Years ago when German persecution was rampant, many Germans fled their country and sought refuge in Chile. This quaint, spotlessly clean village still carried the cultural influence of their native country. Many of the houses were decorated with gingerbread trim, while others conveyed the architectural designs of Swiss influence. We were surprised to find the churches and barns of the community were built much like those here in Pennsylvania and in other areas where Germans also immigrated. Their stone-fenced farms, yard fences, and gates all were evidence of their heritage.

One of the towns had erected a monument depicting the settling of these people. The monument was a young man carrying an axe and a shovel, with his wife by his side carrying a small baby, while a little boy clutched her skirt. This monument moved my emotions as I was reminded of how many of us are descendants of immigrants who traveled to America to escape similar circumstances of persecution. My mother's heritage is rooted in Holland, Germany, and Switzerland, while my father's ancestors came from Scotland and Ireland.

At the end of the trail was yet another pleasant surprise. Off in the distance there was a lodge and restaurant to accommodate weary travelers. After a refreshing drink, we walked down a set of steep steps behind the rustic lodge to the edge of the Pacific Ocean inlet. There was a flower garden and landscaped embankment that was gorgeous! Flowers grew prolifically from the moisture off the ocean. It was a tranquil place! We reveled in the beauty and peacefulness of the Pacific, just as its name implies.

Osvaldo whispered, "I want you to hear something. Listen." The silence was phenomenal! Not a sound could be heard—no singing of birds, croaking of frogs, or chirping insects. Just complete silence. The serenity of those moments was awesome. We looked out over the motionless water of the inlet, beholding the beauty. I will never forget this place where we could actually hear silence, for it was heavenly. It seemed as if the whole world had stopped to hear a whisper from her Creator.

We spent a day traveling with the family to the Andes Mountains. This was a fun time for Paulina and Connie as they played along the streams and exercised among the six-to-eight foot cacti on the hillsides. The scenery was magnificent! Now I could understand why Osvaldo looked at me strangely when I had shown him our tallest peak of the Tuscarora mountains back in Pennsylvania. He had commented, "Mother, they are only hills compared to our Andes." How true that is!

Near the end of the week, we traveled west to Vina del Mar, Chile's most famous resort. Osvaldo had made reservations at Mira Mar, a hotel used by government dignitaries in Chile. Security was tight that night, with soldiers standing by each entrance. The hotel jutted out into the ocean. It was difficult to sleep because I wanted to enjoy every moment as the waves rushed in and out past our windows.

The day for our good-byes came all too soon. The whole family took us to the airport to see us off. The girls, both in Paul's arms, clinging like two little magnets, verified that he truly had taken well to the grandfather roll.

Our family was richly blessed to share our home and love with this fine Chilean lad. Now in turn, he had given us a wonderful vacation with his family. As the plane rose through the clouds and headed for the United States, we praised God for these days of enrichment. The day came when Osvaldo's children learned to speak English, a requirement for this trip, and they came to visit Grandfather and Grandma in Pennsylvania. God has rich rewards for each of us who share our love with others!

Chapter 24

Lord of the Valleys

Life afforded us a new challenge as my mother's health deteriorated. As a result, my stepfather did most of the housecleaning. We children had been going to the house daily to take food and to provide some personal care for almost a year. In July of 1986, she had a debilitating stroke. Hospitalization and nursing home care was required for seven months. Her therapy seemed to be doing nothing for her recovery. When I arrived for my daily afternoon visits, I often found her waiting for me with her nighties in her lap and tears in her eyes. She had lost her ability to speak, but I understood she was asking me to take her home. How my heart ached to do just that.

Having spent some time in coronary care several years before, I needed to exercise care for my heart condition. I was hesitant to tackle the task of caring for my mother at home. My faith was not strong enough, and I saw too many giants that made me a grasshopper in my own eyes. However, deep in my heart I knew God could supernaturally give me the strength and health needed to care for Mother. This wrestling would not let me go. Finally I decided to ask advice from my doctor during my periodic checkup. He informed me that I would not be able to keep up with the continual demands of bathing, feeding, and personal care Mother would need.

Paul and I earnestly sought a word from the Lord. One afternoon at a women's meeting, I asked for prayer about my burden.

While Loretta Martin, a minister's wife, was praying with me, she stopped and said, "The Lord has a message for you. God is going to give you a peace, and when it comes, you will know it is His will for you to care for your mother." Immediately I sensed a deep, settled knowledge that God would be with me in this time of trouble, and His peace settled over me. Day after day it remained.

I am sharing this chapter of my life to encourage some who may be struggling with this challenge. I encourage you to go before the Lord for His direction. Every case needs to be evaluated separately.

Paul agreed to support my decision and stand by me as much as possible, for he also had a job away from home. However, we first wanted to have a conference with my family to see what each of them could do to help us with her care. It was a serious time for us as we looked through the eyes of love and appreciation for all she had done in giving us a life of devotion. My brother Kenneth agreed to come once a month while we went to the Full Gospel Business Men's Fellowship and banquet. Vernon and his wife Louise volunteered to relieve me every third Sunday so I could go to church and Sunday school. Annabelle and Tom visited each Saturday night, and Richard came most every evening to feed her dinner. With God's help we would all make a good team!

We asked the nursing home administrator to hold Mother's room for two weeks until we felt confident with her care. The Lord helped us find two ladies to serve as stand-by persons when I had doctor's appointments or needed a day of bed rest. Doris Snyder, LPN, and Lois Rosenberry were a wonderful blessing. Mother loved both of these women dearly, as they treated her with much patience and love. My husband was a tremendous help and so patient about all the changes that needed to be made in our home. He even cared for her alone at night during the five days I was hospitalized for throat surgery.

We brought her to our house in February. As I knelt by her bed for prayer the first night, she lifted my hand to her lips to kiss me. I knew it was a token of her love and gratitude. The only convenient room in our home for her care was our one and only living room. She was content when she was near us. It was not an ideal situation, but everyone learned to respect her spot to give her a degree of privacy and quietness. Our stepfather's children looked after his care during this time. He came to visit or was brought by his son Ray until his health failed and he entered a nursing home.

In May Paul was trimming evergreens from a stepladder when he fell, fracturing his back in three places. The next several weeks were very demanding, and someone jokingly wondered if I was starting a nursing home. Occasionally some of our friends would stop by with a casserole or dessert and encouragement. Each reminded me that "this too will pass." A few days after the accident, our close friends, Myron and Ethel Hawbaker, visited. As they were leaving I pulled Ethel back into the house. I put my head on her shoulder and let out my weariness and frustration in one great flood of tears. I was so grateful for such a friend with whom I could release all my pent-up emotions. Paul's recovery went well, and I found his presence around the house for the next five months a source of encouragement.

Mother had given me years of tender care, and it was now time for our roles to be reversed. We had many enjoyable times, which outweighed the difficult ones. She liked to spend time with me in the kitchen, watching me from her wheelchair as I prepared meals. Painting had been her favorite pastime. One day as I was painting, she reached for the brush and smiled. As she dipped the brush in the paint, hoping to improve my artistic efforts, nothing but a blotch was made on the canvas. I will never forget the look of disappointment in her expression. This beautiful talent had also vanished from the stroke that destroyed her motor skills. She was a well-known artist with paintings hanging in the local courthouse, bank, church, and many homes. Some of her talent remains as several of her children and grandchildren have inherited this talent. Through us, her life continues on!

The peace of God still lingered in my spirit as we learned to depend on Him and take one day at a time. Each day was a walk of faith for our whole family, and we found it a rewarding time as we pulled together for Mother's care. Jesus was Lord of this valley!

When I think of valleys, I am inspired by my friend, Ava Marsh, who has blessed my life with her magnificent example of commitment. She has worked as a missionary to the Navajo Indians in Arizona and New Mexico. Each year she came to our area for a month of rest and deputation work. While in our community, she stayed in the home of a friend of mine, Jane Christman. I sometimes chauffeured her to meetings. During these drives she shared much about her work with me, both struggles and blessings. When Ava and some of her family originally felt the call to work with the Navajo, they were not sure just where they were to be stationed; they headed west in a bus. After several breakdowns they found themselves in Navajo territory with a bus too costly to fix. In that very territory an elderly minister had been praying that God would send him someone to help evangelize the Indians. The name of the place was Wheatfields, Arizona. From Ava's description, the fields were indeed white unto harvest.

Ava's bus was transformed into her home, and that is where she spent the next seven years of her life. Although some of her family chose to move on to other places of ministry, her love for these people and her desire to see them liberated from the bondage of sin and alcohol overrode her desire for the comforts of a better way of life. An inspiration of commitment, she presents her life as a living sacrifice: she has endured cold, heat, persecution, attacks on her life, loneliness, and scarcity of food in this remote area. She has traveled many miles alone over rugged territory in her Cherokee wagon. Ava has little of this world's goods but is laying up treasures in Heaven "where neither moth nor rust doth corrupt, and where thieves do not break through nor steal" (Mt. 6:20).

During the last part of Isaac's seminary studies, he served as an associate minister in a churchplanting work in Fredericksburg, Virginia. After serving there for some time, he and Rosanna began to feel the call to return to foreign missions. They contacted the mission board and learned there was an opening for a couple in Caracas, Venezuela.

Another student on campus learned of Isaac's interest in Venezuela and offered to show them slides from a short-term mission to that country. While viewing the slides, they saw pictures of the capital city of Caracas. They saw the city, which is 12 miles long and two and a half miles wide, built between two very high mountains. The Holy Spirit reminded them of the vision that had been shared with them several years before. Just before Isaac's graduation from Elim, the students had a time of fasting and prayer for future direction in ministry. Was this the special revelation God had given the man in the vision of Isaac and Rosanna ministering in a large city surrounded by mountains? Could it be Caracas was where God was calling?

In their spirits they felt a quickening that this was a confirmation of where God would have them go. After seminary graduation Isaac was ordained, and they were commissioned by their home church in Pennsylvania for the Venezuelan assignment.

They left August 19, 1988, for San Jose, Costa Rica, to attend language school for refresher courses. Having them go again, this time with the boys, left an ache in my heart. Yet we were confident this was God's will for them, and we wanted them to be obedient to that call.

Again we looked forward to their letters, which told us of their many interesting experiences in Costa Rica. They made new friends at the language school who were also preparing for destinations in Peru and other countries in Central and South America. Nathaniel was in the third grade and Stephen in kindergarten. One day Stephen came home from school exclaiming, "Mommy, Mommy, something wonderful happened to me today!" Rosanna saw the excitement in his face and inquired what happened.

Stephen responded, "God talked to me today, and He said, 'I will be with you wherever you go.' " This news comforted us tremendously. It was a wonderful joy to know God was putting faith and trust in the heart of one so small, for even at that tender age one can develop the relationship spoken of in John 10:3-4.

...and the sheep hear his voice: and he calleth his own sheep by name, and leadeth them out. And when he putteth

forth his own sheep, he goeth before them, and the sheep
follow him: for they know his voice (John 10:3-4).

A week before Isaac, Rosanna, and the boys left, Mother was hospitalized following another stroke with multiple complications. After returning from the airport the day of the children's departure, we went immediately to the hospital to learn the doctor's prognosis was for her imminent departure from this life. Out of pure exhaustion, I decided to go home, get some rest, and return early the next morning. How could so much stress be packed into so little time?

I was leaving the house the next morning about nine o'clock when the doctor telephoned to say Mother had just died. I felt saddened that none of us were with her at this time, but we were thankful she had won her last needed victory here on earth. We had no question that she had been attended by angels who had carried her to her heavenly mansion. These 18 months had been among our most rewarding times of ministry, and helpful in our grieving process by knowing we had provided her quality time with the family.

Several months went by, then another sadness gripped our family. Rosanna gave birth prematurely to Andrew Julian. Although perfect and healthy, at only two pounds, he had little chance to survive the limited health care at the children's hospital in San Jose. Paul and I searched frantically for leads to a medical airlift to Miami. Arrangements were finally made, but his condition never warranted the flight. The day, January 10, that they were to fly into Caracas, they instead flew back to the States for the baby's burial. We turned to the Lord with our many questions. Had satan stepped in to discourage them and cause them to turn back from their assignment? Perhaps this was one of the trials the apostle described in First Peter.

Beloved, think it not strange concerning the fiery trial
which is to try you, as though some strange thing happened
unto you: but rejoice, inasmuch as ye are partakers of

Christ's sufferings; that, when His glory shall be revealed,
ye may be glad also with exceeding joy (1 Peter 4:12-13).

Three weeks later, they arrived in Caracas. They faced a difficult assignment, for they were sent to work with a church with overwhelming problems. It was a time of sowing in tears as satan tried every trick in his book to destroy the saints and their church. However, the time came when they were able to reap with joy and see the fruit of their labors. With faith, they pressed on by long periods of united prayer and fasting with others in a new fellowship in the town of Charallave.

The Christian walk provides more than valley experiences, for we are often granted mountaintops of blessing. Most importantly, we must keep our grip on the One who has control of every phase of our lives.

Chapter 25

In Satan's Sieve

Little did I realize when the Lord instructed me to write that I would need years of experience to accumulate what He wanted me to share of His love and power. After two years of spasmodic writing, I began to feel guilty that I was not getting a manuscript ready for publication. There were always people who needed ministry or speaking appointments to prepare for. It was virtually impossible to have time, or even feel the fervor to write. The needs of the ministry at hand always seemed more urgent.

I called my friend Rachel, who had been with me the morning the Lord directed me to write, and shared my concern. She authoritatively said, "Betty Jane, God has so much more to teach you that He would have you write about."

I knew it was the Holy Spirit speaking through her, and I began to rest in this prophetic word. Some years I have written very little such as the time I cared for my mother. However, I always tried to keep my mind in tune to the Lord for truths that might be a blessing.

Last summer at a church conference, the keynote speaker was awakened early in the morning. The Lord showed him several faces, and for each one of these he was given a message. When he came to the pulpit, he announced that he had a responsibility to discharge before his sermon. As he scanned the faces in the audience, one by one he picked out these four people, his finger pointing to each of us.

I vividly remember his words: "The Lord says, 'It is now time for you to finish the work I have commissioned you to do.' " There was no question in my mind; I knew He meant my writing. The Lord created quiet periods of time with a compulsive urgency to write; a satisfaction accompanied the desire.

I want to share what the Lord has taught me concerning spiritual warfare. Even though Paul and I had encountered some work in deliverance earlier, there was yet much to learn through personal experience. I truly believe God wants His people to know how to do battle against the devil, for in the last days satan will unleash his power, knowing that his time is short. Lately ministers and their families, missionaries, and other Christians are coming under attack. I believe God would have Christians understand this warfare, not only for ourselves but also to help those around us. Unified effort brings greater power. When we are weak, it is often difficult to pray; and we need others to be our prayer warriors.

For spiritual battle it is imperative for us to understand the cost of our redemption through Jesus' shed blood. It is of utmost importance that we understand we are robed in His righteousness and adopted into the family of God with all its entitlements. This is our divine legacy. In Isaiah 61:10 we read about that robing:

I will greatly rejoice in the Lord, my soul shall be joyful in my God; for He hath clothed me with the garments of salvation, He hath covered me with the robe of righteousness, as a bridegroom decketh himself with ornaments, and as a bride adorneth herself with her jewels.

Furthermore, in Romans we read of our adoption into the family of God.

For as many as are led by the Spirit of God, they are the sons of God. For ye have not received the spirit of bondage again to fear; but ye have received the Spirit of adoption, whereby we cry, Abba, Father. The Spirit itself beareth witness with our spirit, that we are the children of God: and if children, then heirs; heirs of God, and joint-heirs with

Christ; if so be that we suffer with Him, that we may be also glorified together (Romans 8:14-17).

We plan and expect to use our earthly inheritance from our parents. The heavenly Father has planned for our spiritual inheritance and expects us to use it as joint-heirs with Jesus Christ. This includes His power and authority to combat the forces of evil. We do not pray for the Lord to push satan from us, but we need to exercise authority and power ourselves against his attacks.

At the onset of Jesus' ministry, He was confronted with temptation by satan in the wilderness. Jesus battled this foe with the Word of God. This is our pattern for spiritual warfare. We need to know the Word of God in our head and heart and use it against satan when he attacks.

For whatsoever is born of God overcometh the world: and this is the victory that overcometh the world, even our faith. Who is he that overcometh the world, but he that believeth that Jesus is the Son of God? (1 John 5:4-5)

Satan soon confronted us. It had been almost a year since we had seen Rosanna and the family. We longed to see them, the country of Venezuela, their apartment, and we wanted to learn to know the people of the church in Caracas. We decided to leave in November to spend Thanksgiving with them and return in two weeks. It was wonderful to be together again, and we were surprised to see how much the boys had grown. We had ten good days of visiting.

We found the culture in Venezuela to be very different from that in Honduras or Chile. Their economy boomed because of the mass production of oil, until their oil market collapsed. People from surrounding countries flooded into Venezuela for jobs. Many entered illegally from Columbia and squatted on the hillsides of the mountains around the city. These areas are called *ranchos* and are areas of high crime. Even the police do not enter these masses of pitiful-looking homes built with scraps of material and seemingly stacked upon one another.

I personally do not care for the noise and traffic of city life. Because the Spanish people love music and parties, they use every occasion to have one. The city is a maze of concrete with high-rise apartments. Many streets are littered with debris, and walls are decorated with obnoxious graffiti. However, the need for these multitudes of humanity to learn of Jesus Christ is tantamount. As the crowds thronged the streets, I wondered what purpose they may have in life. One needs to be constantly alert for pickpockets and other similar dangers. The children's apartment, though small, was adequate and a haven from the tulmult, after entering through the four locks for security.

Our second Sunday night in Venezuela we shared our testimony at the church. One of their members, a young pediatrician, had trouble with his marriage. He called Isaac for an appointment for counseling, hoping to bring a reconciliation between himself and his Jewish wife who had returned to her parents that very day. He brought with him two other women from the church. These women followed after him for financial aid to support their ambition to hold revivals in some village away from the city. Because they both had small children and one an unsaved husband, they were unlikely candidates for God to call for such ministry. They were noted for bringing discord within the congregation through the misuse of spiritual gifts. Whether their desire was a real call to serve or a deception from the devil is not mine to judge.

The doctor spoke broken English, which the women apparently did not understand. During counseling we admonished him that it was not wise to have these women in his company and noted it was natural that his wife would be upset. After some further conversation, the four of us began to pray for wisdom. During this prayer I had a "word of knowledge"—*Hinduism*.

I asked him what this meant to him, and he said he had some involvement in this religion in his search for Christ. I told him there was no way I could have known this since I knew nothing about him, and by this revelation we believed that God wanted to free him from this bondage. He asked that we pray for him to be released from this influence on his life.

We prayed only a short while until he began to choke and cough and go through sounds as if he were going to vomit. We knew this manifestation was from demon spirits. We commanded them to come out in the name of Jesus. The struggle lasted for a few minutes, and finally he was set free by the mighty power of God. He testified of his inner struggle and that at first he was not sure that he was willing to give full control to the Lord. When he made his decision to yield completely to Christ, he said he felt the demons leave and he had the peace of Jesus sweep over him. He sat motionless in his chair, relaxed in the love of God. Finally, he said he wanted to call his office and have the secretary cancel his afternoon appointments. He wanted to go home and bask in the precious peace that was sweeping over his soul.

The two women were standing by and wondered to Isaac if we had ever seen this happen before. He assured them that we had and that they were to give all praise to God and not to man.

Satan uses many tactics in his attempts to destroy any emissary of Christ and to block the effectiveness of that person. From the time of satan's fall, this was his strategy and I would be no exception.

> *And the Lord said, Simon, Simon, behold, Satan hath desired to have you, that he may sift you as wheat: but I have prayed for thee, that thy faith fail not: and when thou art converted, strengthen thy brethren* (Luke 22:31-32).

The following day I had a bowel blockage. I had never experienced intestinal trouble. What was taking place? Isaac and Paul anointed me. The next morning I was in intense pain and was admitted to the hospital. This was the beginning of a traumatic experience of spiritual warfare. Several doctors were called, none of whom could speak English; therefore it was impossible for me to give my medical history. Isaac interpreted as much as he could, and I was given something to allay my pain.

Several hours later another doctor was put on my case. He could speak English! What a blessing! He explained to me what was happening and what tests would need to be done. The nurses spoke only Spanish. What a dilemma I found myself in! By the next morning my temperature was elevated. I had a ruptured colon with peritonitis. I learned that Dr. Fernandez was known to be the most skilled surgeon in Venezuela. What a provision the Lord had made. Rosanna traveled across the city by taxi and was with me as much of the time as possible.

When I awoke from surgery, I was in the Intensive Care Unit. The room was air-conditioned to approximately 60 degrees. The nurses were working with coats and blankets around their shoulders. With an elevated temperature, I was chilled beyond measure as I lay there in my disposable paper gown, which covered only the trunk of my body. I had only one blanket for cover. I clasped my arms to my body and shook profusely to indicate I wanted more cover. But instead I got the bath of my life! The nurse poured pitcher after pitcher of cold water over my now naked body. My teeth were chattering. I cried out to the Lord, "Only you can keep me from getting pneumonia in this place."

Apparently they did this to bring temperature down, and whether my fever warranted the many pitchers of water, or whether the nurse was being sure she gave this North American woman a regal bath, I will never know. The cleaning lady stood by with her mop and bucket, spewing out Spanish in a rapid torrent. I think my ears were fortunate at that time that the language was foreign to me, for I am sure she was cursing the nurse for the terrible mess she had to clean up.

Later, I was moved to a large, private room on the seventh floor. The Lord arranged for me to have this room. The doctors' offices were on the twelfth floor. The hospital was operated by Catholics and was immaculately clean. In my room there was a narrow padded bench for sitting or sleeping accommodations for family members. Rosanna or Paul was allowed to stay with me all but two nights. What a comfort they were! Ephesians 3:13 became special to me, "Wherefore I desire that ye faint not at my tribulations for you, which is your glory." I had an unusual sense of the presence of the Lord.

The week before I entered the hospital, I had attended a Women's Aglow Bible study and met some of the sisters there. Several of them came to the hospital to visit, bringing flowers and encouragement. The Lord gave me a Scripture from First Thessalonians 5:18, "In every thing give thanks: for this is the will of God in Christ Jesus concerning you." I knew that He had some special purpose for all that was happening to me. However, I did not fully understand what it was all about at that time. But with the peace of His presence and this Scripture, I knew He would see me through. Several of the Aglow sisters gave me this same Scripture when they came to visit. Giving thanks for a colostomy was not an easy assignment, but I did have the hope of having it reversed in several months.

Dr. Fernandez, a friendly and sensitive gentleman, continually impressed me with the fact that my recovery was exceptional. Back at Rosanna's apartment hung a wall motto, *"Todo es posible para Dios."* Translated, it reads "Everything is possible with God." Not every day was a good day, as Rosanna patiently taught me to care for my new attachment. I constantly felt that there was a war raging within me. However, I recalled Job and how God had allowed this righteous man to be tested by satan. Even as Job was in satan's sieve, I also identified with the permissive will of God as spoken of in Job 13:15a, "Though He slay me, yet will I trust in Him." I prayed that God would be merciful to me.

The Lord was both merciful and faithful. We flew home after six weeks, on December 31, 1989. I was still quite weak and was helped by a wheelchair waiting for me at the airport terminals. I feel that the many prayers of those back home had greatly helped me to win the battle and triumph over satan. When news reached the States, there must have been a great networking of calls for prayer for me and my husband. How I rejoice for the love of family and friends who prayed for me in this hour of need. In Venezuela, as well as many other countries that are steeped in witchcraft, it is not uncommon to be cursed and not win the victory. When God's power is evidenced in a life, satan becomes furious and will do what he can to stop the work and ministry of that person.

The lesson for me to learn was how very real my enemy is and to continually practice the use of God's power and authority that was shown to me during the vision in which I was robed in Christ's blood. I experienced this so that I could see the importance of standing in the gap for others in the onslaught of spiritual battles. Arriving home by no means meant my battle was over. In March, I had my reversal surgery. For the surgeon this proved to be six hours of intense work to divide my intestines that had grown together as a result of the peritonitis. I vividly remember fighting for every breath and commanding the devil to go in the name of Jesus.

The second day after surgery, I learned that when I am weak, then am I strong (see 2 Cor. 12:10). Heavily sedated for pain, I was vomiting and intensely weak. A spirit-filled woman came to see me. I had not seen Julie for several years. However, she told me that God had sent her to the hospital to pray with me. She could scarcely have left the parking lot when a young man came into my room for prayer. I knew and loved him dearly. He was overcome with fear and desperately needed deliverance. Something powerful happened within my spirit, and I was amazed with the authority I was given in those moments for ministry. When he left I was overwhelmed with the seriousness of his situation and asked the Lord to please send someone to covenant in prayer with me.

I was astonished to see Frank Heckman, a dear friend and prayer warrior from 50 miles away, step into the room within five minutes of my prayer. How wonderful it was to sense the power of his prayer of rejuvenation and experience the promise of Isaiah 65:24, "And it shall come to pass, that before they call, I will answer; and while they are yet speaking, I will hear."

I had to have major surgery again in November. I had many hours to sit and reflect on God's goodness. However, many times entering into the Lord's presence was difficult, for often there seemed to be a dark wall or heavy cloud. A heaviness pressed against me with waves of discouragement. Would this feeling never cease? It was now 15 months since satan's initial attack on my body.

In March of 1990, our church was having revival. I felt particularly impressed to fast and pray that day. I was not aware that the evening's message was to be on prayer and fasting. I was blessed that the Lord led me to do this, for I fully believe that this is essential to be victorious in spiritual warfare. Since it was winter, it was dark when we parked our car. When church was over, we found a beautiful white dove sitting on the hood of our car with her tail feathers just touching the windshield. Paul said, "Isn't this unusual, I wonder how she got here?" With awe I whispered, "The dove of peace!" For several minutes we stood admiring her beauty, realizing this was a supernatural phenomenon. As we got into the car, she flew off into the night. For days these words kept ringing in my heart with thanksgiving. God had now pushed my foe beyond his limits. The wall and the cloud had been moved back. Once again I could enter into His sweet presence. Hallelujah!

Since that time we have encountered many who are battling with the forces of darkness and come to us seeking help. We feel we have learned valuable lessons through this experience and are better equipped to help others through their battles.

Four years later we returned to Venezuela to see our family again. We desired to see the children and meet the people where God was pouring out His Spirit in revival. We learned to love the people from the church in Charallave and found it difficult to say good-bye to them.

I close this chapter from a reference in the Book of Isaiah 26:3-4: "Thou wilt keep him in perfect peace, whose mind is stayed on Thee: because he trusteth in Thee. Trust ye in the Lord for ever: for in the Lord Jehovah is everlasting strength."

Chapter 26

Sound the Trumpet

With joy and thanksgiving I reminisce over a life filled with the goodness of Almighty God. The blessings have far outweighed the toil, pain, sadness, and difficulties that have been a part of our life.

Many changes have transpired during these years. The economic world has drastically changed. As a private secretary for an electric company, my wage was $20 a week, with $1.50 a week raise after six months. Now many persons make that much an hour. There was a time when we thrilled to dash outside to watch a single-engine plane flying overhead. Now we board a jumbo jet and fly thousands of miles to visit other continents. Medical technology has made great strides. The discovery of antibiotics and new medications has saved lives and expanded life expectancy beyond what we dared dream of years ago.

My first meals were cooked and baked on a wood or coal-fueled stove, which gave off tremendous heat in summertime. How I appreciate electricity for lighting, cooking, refrigeration, laundry, air-conditioning, and yes, my wonderful microwave! I am thankful that it is no longer necessary to dry and can fruits and vegetables, for fresh ones are in the supermarkets from across our country or imported so that we now have an abundant variety and supply to choose from all year long. The fancy room to bathe and powder our nose has eliminated the "outhouse." However, instead of taking a leisure walk down a country lane enjoying the fragrance of honeysuckles, we get our exercise on a treadmill that takes us nowhere fast. Once we learned what was happening in the community by word of mouth or the telephone, if one was fortunate enough to have a line built by your property. Now we push a few buttons on our remote control, and from our La-Z-boy chair we can see what is happening around the world.

People were once considered influential and respected for hard work; now they are classified as "blue-collar workers." Many children are no longer wanted and are aborted while dogs and cats receive luxurious care. I have lived to see narrow gravel roads become six and eight-lane superhighways. Are these inventions a blessing, or a curse to snare us to the god of pleasure and ease? Spirituality has not kept pace with our technology. What is happening to God's beautiful world?

The Holy Spirit is reminding me of a prophecy recorded in the Book of Daniel 12:4, "But thou, O Daniel, shut up the words, and seal the book, even to the time of the end: many shall run to and fro, and knowledge shall be increased." Never have we witnessed the types of running to and fro we have today, and knowledge has certainly increased. Many of the inventions and much of the knowledge have improved our life, but at the same time we have seen man worship the creature more than the Creator (see Rom. 1:25).

I believe with all my heart that the time for the Lord to return for the Church, His Bride, is close at hand. I marvel at so many changes. I am awed by why God would choose us, ordinary persons, to use as instruments of His love and and why He would reveal so many truths to our hearts.

I feel so indebted to the Father, Son, and Holy Spirit. The songwriter has said, "Jesus paid a debt he did not owe, and I owed a debt I could not pay." When I was a small girl and someone would ask, "What is your favorite Scripture?" I would recite Romans 12:1, "I beseech you therefore, brethren, by the mercies of God, that ye present your bodies a living sacrifice, holy, acceptable unto

God, which is your reasonable service." But as I grew older, I realized that the following verse could not be separated from the one before it. "And be not conformed to this world: but be ye transformed by the renewing of your mind, that ye may prove what is that good, and acceptable, and perfect, will of God" (Rom. 12:2). His consuming love requires my sacrifice and devotion, and I strive to comprehend what is the breadth, and length, and depth, and height of the love of Christ (see Eph. 3:18-19) so that I can be filled with that love.

I have discovered that God is an all-sufficient, everlasting source, and what He supplies can continually flow from us like a fountain of love to our fellowman. Some time ago I heard this song that relates the desire of my heart. I wish I could give tribute to the composer of the music and the words to this song. However, I have been unable to locate the author.

Let Your Love Flow Through Me

So many folks are lonely,
Oh, Lord they need someone to care.
And when I look about and see them
I can't help making this my prayer.

But when I meet a lost one
Give me all the right words I should say
Oh, help me not be weak or timid,
Their only chance may be with me today.

Chorus
Let your love flow through me,
Let your love flow through me, make me a
Blessing Lord, Wherever I may be
Keep me pure, keep me clean,
So that you might be seen
Let your love, let your love
Flow through me.

It is my heart's desire to sincerely embrace the promise of the Lord in John 7:38. "He that believeth on Me, as the scripture hath said, out of his belly [innermost being] shall flow rivers of living water."

December 31, 1972, we invited guests to our home for a New Year celebration, which included dinner and an evening of fellowship. We gathered around the piano, sang hymns, and had a time of thanksgiving testimonies of the past year. We ended with a season of prayer as we looked forward to the new year.

Early the next morning I was awakened for a most remarkable experience. Like the apostle Paul, I cannot say whether I was in the body or in the spirit. Yet I was very aware that I had been lifted high above the earth, and from this lofty vantage point I beheld the earth beneath. I was enthralled with the magnificence of God's creation as I looked down at the mountains, valleys, rivers, and smaller streams. But as I looked, I realized the Lord had taken me here for a special purpose. I felt His presence and asked, "Lord, why are You showing me this?"

As my eyes focused on the beauty, something catastrophic happened. The mountains crumbled, and the rivers moved out of their courses. My vocabulary can find no words to describe the horror of it. I felt I would die if I continued to see what was taking place. I began to weep and the Lord said, "I have a message for you to proclaim, **tell My people to be ready!**"

The next thing I remember, I was sitting back in bed. I was awestruck with where I had been and what I had seen. Then the Lord spoke again, "What you have just seen can be found in the prophecy of Ezekiel chapter 38." I hurried for my Bible and opened it to read:

> *Thus saith the Lord God; In that day when My people of Israel dwelleth safely, shalt thou not know it? And thou shalt come from thy place out of the north parts, thou, and many people with thee, all of them riding upon horses, a great company, and a mighty army: and thou shalt come up against My people of Israel, as a cloud to cover the land; it shall be in the latter days…. And it shall come to pass at*

the same time when Gog [presumably some northern coun-
try] *shall come against the land of Israel, saith the Lord
God, that My fury shall come up in My face. ...Surely in
that day there shall be a great shaking in the land of Israel;
so that the fishes of the sea, and the fowls of the heaven,
and the beasts of the field, and all creeping things that
creep upon the earth, and all the men that are upon the face
of the earth, shall shake at My presence, and the mountains
shall be thrown down, and the steep places shall fall, and
every wall shall fall to the ground. And I will call for a
sword against him throughout all My mountains, saith the
Lord God: every man's sword shall be against his brother.
And I will plead against him with pestilence and with
blood; and I will rain upon him, and upon his bands, and
upon the many people that are with him, an overflowing
rain, and great hailstones, fire, and brimstone. Thus will I
magnify Myself; and sanctify Myself; and I will be known
in the eyes of many nations, and they shall know that I am
the Lord* (Ezekiel 38:14b-23).

I do not claim to be a prophetess or to understand prophecy, but
I feel that God will come for His Bride the Church before this
event takes place. The Lord has given me opportunity to share this
message with thousands of people. I pray that the Holy Spirit will
give understanding as I sound the trumpet, and that we, His people, will lift up our heads, for our redemption draweth nigh (see
Lk. 21:28).

We are celebrating our forty-seventh wedding anniversary today, March 5, 1996, as we put the final touches to this manuscript.
This book is a gift of love and praise to our Lord Jesus.

Shannon's family continue their work in Maine. Their oldest
son Marvin is married to Ruby Smith of Bowdoinham, Maine.
They have made us the proud great-grandparents of Maxwell
Negley.

Isaac and Rosanna and the boys have returned to the States for
Nathaniel and Stephen's schooling, instead of sending them to a

boarding school near the Columbian border. Isaac is presently pastor at the Dry Run Church of the Brethren.

Bill and Katrina are serving the Lord and enjoying their new home in Spotsylvania, Virginia, where Katrina teaches art in the public schools. She has been my avid encourager throughout the process of writing this book in addition to providing the artwork.

We praise God for continued health and strength. Even though the years are diminishing our vitality and the quickness of our steps, our enthusiasm for serving our great and wonderful Lord Jesus Christ remains. He continues to shower us wtih His amazing riches. Therefore, our love and devotion as His servants to mankind in this hurting world are our delight.

May the love and power of God abide with all who read this book. May you be inspired to deeper depths of commitment and know the joy and rewards of a consecrated walk in the Spirit.

All glory, honor, and praise to the Father, Son, and Holy Ghost who has allowed our eyes to behold glimpses of His glory, majesty, and power!

Paul and Betty Jane Negley

William (Bill) and Katrina Negley Reighard

Isaac and Rosanna Burkholder
From left to right: Stephen and Nathaniel

Shannon and Marian Negley
From left to right: Darrell, Marvin and Ruby
with Maxwell, and Lee